SMALL PIECES LOOSELY JOINED

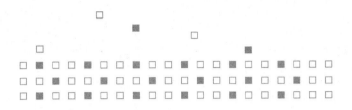

DAVID WEINBERGER

SMALL PIECES LOOSELY JOINED

{ *How the Web Shows Us
Who We Really Are* }

THE PERSEUS PRESS
A Member of the Perseus Books Group

The Perseus Press
A Member of the Perseus Books Group
Originally published in the United States by Perseus Publishing, 2002

Printed in the United Kingdom.

Text design by Jeff Williams

Set in 11-point Simonici Garamond by the Perseus Books Group.

A Cataloging-in-Publication record for this book is available from the British Library.
ISBN 1–903985-36–6

1 2 3 4 5 6 7 8 9 10—06 05 04 03 02

CONTENTS

PREFACE

IN LATE 1993, one of the programmers at the software company where I was vice president of strategic marketing called me into his office. "You have to see this," he said, pointing to his computer screen, standing as I sat, drumming his fingers anxiously on his thighs. There was an ugly gray document in an ugly window labeled "Mosaic." In the middle of the ugly black text was a phrase, underlined and in bright blue. "It's a link," my friend said. He clicked on it, and a new document took its place. The document might well have been titled "Your Company's New Product Is Doomed." I rounded up as many other members of the management team as I could find and brought them in to see what I had seen, and watched the blood drain from their faces as it undoubtedly had from mine.

It's not that we were shocked by the idea of links. Quite the contrary. We had recently launched a product that let users publish their documents online and embed links in them. Plus, our software had capabilities far beyond those of Mosaic. As we stared at the programmer's screen, we reminded ourselves of those differences: publishers could control the layout of the page, could embed graphics of many sorts, and could use multiple columns. We also had a powerful set of tools for creating the documents in the first place, automatically building hyperlinked indexes and tables of contents. So, this little Mosaic viewer wasn't a real threat. Oh, it was a nice enough toy, but the big-time corporations we were dealing with—aircraft manufacturers, pharmaceutical companies, multinationals that practically had their own governments—wouldn't be satisfied with such a dinky little piece of software.

Thus did denial set in. That dinky browser, the progenitor of Netscape, may have lacked the bells and whistles of our software, but it had something from the start that our software would never have: openness. With our software, a publisher could embed a link from one document to another, but the publisher had to own both documents. That's fine if you're putting together a set of aircraft maintenance manuals and you want to make all the cross references active, so that clicking on one brings up the page to which it's referring. But those links had to be compiled into the system. Once the document was published, no more links could be added except by recompiling the document. And, most important, the only people who could add new links were those working for the publisher. If you were an aircraft mechanic who had discovered some better ways to clean a fuel line, you had no way to publish your page with our system and no way to link it to the appropriate page in the official manual.

The Web, on the other hand, breaks the traditional publishing model. The old model is about control: a team works on a document, is responsible for its content and format, and releases it to the public when it's been certified as done. Once

it's published, no one can change it except the original publisher. The Web ditches that model, with all its advantages as
well as its drawbacks, and says instead, "You have something to
say? Say it. You want to respond to something that's been said?
Say it and link to it. You think something is interesting? Link to
it from your home page. And you never have to ask anyone's
permission." Then it adds: "And how long will it take to do
this? I dunno. How fast do you type?" By removing the central
control points, the Web enabled a self-organizing, self-stimu-
lated growth of contents and links on a scale the world has literally never before experienced.

The result is a loose federation of documents—many small
pieces loosely joined. But in what has turned out to be simply
the first cultural artifact and institution the Web has subtly sub-
verted, the interior structure of documents has changed, not
just the way they are connected to one another. The Web has
blown documents apart. It treats tightly bound volumes like a
collection of ideas—none longer than can fit on a single
screen—that the reader can consult in the order she or he
wants, regardless of the author's intentions. It makes links
beyond the document's covers an integral part of every document. What once was literally a tightly bound entity has been
ripped into pieces and thrown into the air.

What the Web has done to documents it is doing to just
about every institution it touches. The Web isn't primarily
about replacing atoms with bits so that we can, for example,
shop online or make our supply chains more efficient. The Web
isn't even simply empowering groups, such as consumers, that
have traditionally had the short end of the stick. Rather, the
Web is changing our understanding of what puts things

together in the first place. We live in a world that works well if the pieces are stable and have predictable effects on one another. We think of complex institutions and organizations as being like well-oiled machines that work reliably and almost serenely so long as their subordinate pieces perform their designated tasks. Then we go on the Web, and the pieces are so loosely joined that frequently the links don't work; all too often we get the message (to put it palindromically) "404! Page gap! 404!" But that's okay because the Web gets its value not from the smoothness of its overall operation but from its abundance of small nuggets that point to more small nuggets. And, most important, the Web is binding not just pages but us human beings in new ways. We are the true "small pieces" of the Web, and we are loosely joining ourselves in ways that we're still inventing.

So now you know where this book's title comes from. The subtitle is a different issue. The "unified theory of the Web" it promises is quite similar to the unified theory of physics from which I derived its name—but only in that both are nonexistent.

I toyed with maintaining that my unified theory of the Web is that the Web consists of many small pieces loosely joined. But this would have put it in the same category as Ann Elk's Theory of the Brontosaurus as explained in a Monty Python sketch. After much ahem-ing, John Cleese, as Ms. Elk, pronounces her theory:

> My theory by A. Elk. Brackets Miss, brackets. This theory goes as follows and begins now. All brontosauruses are thin at one end, much thicker in the middle and then thin again at the far end. That is my theory, it is mine, and belongs to me and I own it, and what it is too.[1]

While "The Web consists of many small pieces loosely joined" may be only slightly more helpful than Ann Elk's contribution, this book does suggest a way of thinking about the Web that, although not as rigorous as a unified theory, will, I hope, help drive the conversation deeper. I'm one of those who believe that we can be individuals only because we are members of groups. Our families, our communities, and our culture make us what we are. And once we are what we are, we are still unthinkable outside the groups with whom we live; maroon us on a desert isle, and we'll form an association with a volley ball if we have to. So if a new infrastructure comes along that allows us to connect with everyone else on the planet and to invent new types of connections, this is big news indeed.

Even so, the conversation needs to take one step more. Our social connections until now have almost all been constrained by geography and atoms: the real world. These constraints feel natural to us because that's exactly what they are. They're so natural that they're usually invisible: it's inconspicuously true that we generally have to travel longer to get to places that are farther away; that to be heard at the back of the theater, you have to speak louder; that when a couple moves apart, their relationship changes; that if I give you something, I no longer have it; that our presence in the world is continuous from birth until death. Our every social act implicitly conforms itself to the geographic and material facts of the real world. But the Web is an unnatural world, one we have built for ourselves. The facts of nature drop out of the Web. And so we can see reflected in the Web just how much of our sociality is due not to the nature of the real world but to the nature of ourselves. The Web confronts us with a different sort of brute fact: we are creatures who care about ourselves and the world we share with others; we live within a context of meaning; the world is richer with meaning than we can imagine.

The Web gives us an opportunity to rethink many of our presuppositions about our nature and our world's nature. Only by so doing can we begin to discern why the Web has excited us far beyond reasonable expectation. The hype about the Web hasn't been unwarranted, only misdirected. The conversation I believe we need to have is about what the Web is showing us about ourselves. What is true to our nature and what only looked that way because it was a response to a world that was, until now, the only one we had?

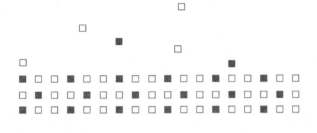

SMALL PIECES LOOSELY JOINED

chapter one

A NEW WORLD

WHEN MICHAEL IAN CAMPBELL used an online alias, no one was suspicious. After all, choosing a name by which you'll be known on the Web is a requirement for using America Online. Known as "Soup81" to his AOL buddies, the eighteen-year-old Campbell was considered a polite, even kind young man in the Florida town where he lived with his mother. At the end of 1999, he had finished his first semester at a community college and was working in a retail store during the day; at night, he pursued his dream by acting in plays at the Cape Coral Cultural Theater. On December 15, he and millions of others were using America Online's "instant messaging" facility to type messages back and forth to their friends old and new. Instant messaging opens a window on your computer screen in which the letters being typed by your conversant show up as they're being typed. It's like watching over the shoulder of someone typing—even the effect of the Delete key is eerily evident—although that person can be thousands of miles away. Indeed, Soup81 was chatting with sixteen-year-old Erin Walton in Colorado, someone he had never met before. He did know something about her, though: eight months earlier, a pair of teenagers had killed thirteen people at Walton's high school, Columbine, in Littleton, Colorado.

After some initial chitchat, Campbell typed a warning onto Walton's screen. Don't go to school the next day, his message said, because "I need to finish what begun [sic] and if you do [go to school] I don't want your blood on my hands."

When Walton, understandably shaken, alerted Columbine's school officials, they closed the school for two days and postponed exams. Three days later, the FBI got a court order in Denver forcing AOL to name the person behind the screen name "Soup81." The agents moved in quickly, questioning Campbell for ninety minutes and taking custody of his computer. A judge ordered Campbell to remain in the county jail without bail until his hearing a few days later.[1]

Campbell's mother blamed this aberrant behavior on the death of her son's father a month earlier. Campbell's lawyer, Ellis Rubin, made up a type of insanity—"Internet intoxication"—to excuse it. But Michael Campbell gave a different explanation. On *The Today Show* a few days later, seemingly trying to puzzle out his own behavior, he said that, as a dedicated actor, he was trying on a role. He was seeing what it would be like to be his favorite actor, John Malkovich.

"Internet intoxication" makes about as much sense as the "Twinkie defense"[2]—Dan White's supposed claim that junk food threw off his moral judgment—but at least it acknowledges that something about the Internet contributed to this event. At the very least, had Campbell met Walton in person, his "channeling" of Malkovich would probably have come off as nothing more than a celebrity impression. The Internet allowed Soup81 to assume a persona and become someone that Michael Ian Campbell wasn't. In fact, Soup81 didn't usually go around threatening people online; this seems to have been an isolated incident. Although Soup81's actions on December 15, 1999, were atypical of the tens of millions of chats that take place every day, it is not at all unusual on the Web for someone to "try on" a personality and to switch personalities from chat room to chat room: behavior that would cause your family to plot an intervention off the Web is the norm on the Web. The very basics of what it means to have a self-identity through time—an "inner" consistency, a core character from which all else springs—are in question on the Web.[3]

Michael Campbell is, of course, an exception, which is why he got onto The Today Show and the other 300–400 million users of the Web did not. And that's why he served four months in a Florida jail as part of a plea bargain that also forbade him from using the Internet for three years. Fortunately, Campbell's story is not typical. But even the typical, everyday world of the Web is more alien than it at first seems. Take something as ordinary as visiting eBay. For example, I recently visited eBay after deciding that a quilt would make a perfect—or at least safe—housewarming present for a friend moving into his first house. . .

I type "quilt" into the page's search field. In about one second (I have a cable modem), eBay shows me a page listing the first 50 of 8,179 items for sale that include the word "quilt" in their titles, including books about quilts, fabric for making quilts, quilt designs, and quilt stencils. Daunted by the 164 pages of listings, I search again, this time for "homemade quilt," and narrow the list to 16. That seems so few that I reconsider my search query and realize that I should probably search for "handmade" quilts, not "homemade" ones. Sure enough, I now find 248 items, listed according to which auctions are going to be over first. "Stunning Handmade Quilt w/Brilliant Colors" is closing in two hours and twenty-five minutes; its opening bid of $159 has attracted no takers. Too expensive for me, and apparently also for people who know more than I do about quilts. "NEW HANDMADE SMALL COLORFUL QUILT" closes three hours after that; four bidders have pushed the price to $26.09. The picture is small but the explanatory text has a homey touch:

> This quilt measures 56x72 and is very colorful. This quilt is new and will last a lifetime. This would be a perfect fathers day gift, or perfect on back of couch. Please e-mail me with any questions. Shipping will be 5.00. Thank you for looking.

Although the eBay page is formulaic, there's enough context for me to make some tentative judgments. The amateurish prose and layout of the page leads me to assume that the seller isn't full-time in the quilt business. But she seems not to have made the quilt herself because there's no mention of how long it took her and no story about why she made it and why she's now giving it up. Maybe this was a housewarming gift she doesn't like and wants to pass on. Could I be wrong about her? Definitely. But in this case it doesn't matter because the price is too far under the $75 I want to pay for this gift. I may be passing up the bargain of the century, but, as a naïve quilt buyer I have to trust the pricing judgments of the other bidders. I go back to the listing of auctions.

Before I can investigate more offerings, my ten-year-old son slams the door and yells up a cheery "Hey-lo!" and I am distracted for the next couple of hours. It's shortly before dinner when I go back to eBay. On page three there's an auction for a red-and-white quilt currently listed at $66. The picture shows a pattern that I think my friend may like; the design can even be construed as a series of Jewish stars if you catch it at the right angle, which my friend will get a kick out of. The text says:

> This is a beautiful quilt made by my Great Aunt. It is in excellent condition. The colors are beautiful. It measures 89x72. Buyer pays $10 shipping and insurance.

The page tells me that the starting price for the piece was $40 and four people have bid on it so far. This is getting interesting. So, I click on the rating next to the seller's name and eBay takes me to a page of comments from people who have done business with her. Four people have rated her, all have rated her excellent, and each has written a one-line comment praising her to the skies. But I've bought from eBay before and I know how this works: after the sale, the seller and buyer each get to write a brief evaluation. Anything less than lavish praise is taken as veiled criticism. Grade inflation has hit eBay.

I didn't win that auction. And although my interactions with eBay were simple, they were based on assumptions that are quite different from my real-world assumptions. I assumed no locality for the seller and the bidders beyond an expectation that they were probably all on the North American continent;

it's possible that some were in other countries, although the complications of the real-world postal system discourage that. But the distancelessness of the Web is just the most obvious of the disconnects between it and the real world. You could even classify them by using some big concepts from the real world, such as space, time, self, and knowledge:

Space. eBay is a Web space that occupies no space. Its "near" and "far" are determined by what's linked to what, and the links are based not on contiguity but on human interest. The geography of the Web is as ephemeral as human interest: eBay pulled together a listings page for me based on my interest in handmade quilts while simultaneously building pages for thousands of others who had other, unpredictable interests. Each of us looked across the space that is eBay and saw a vastly different landscape: mine of quilts, yours of Star Wars memorabilia, someone else's of battery chargers.

Time. Earlier that morning, while waiting for my wife in our town center, I ducked into a store called Ten Thousand Villages that sells world crafts at prices fair to the artisans.[4] For ten minutes I enjoyed being a yuppie among the Chilean rain sticks and the Djembe drums from Burkina Faso. Then I saw my wife through the window, left the store, and closed the door behind me. Real-world time is a series of ticks to which schedules are tied. My time with eBay was different. As I investigated different auctions, placed a bid, and checked back every few hours to see if I'd been outbid, I felt as if I were returning to a story in progress, waiting for me whenever I wanted. I could break off in the middle when, for example, my son came home, and go back when I had the time. The Web is woven of hundreds of millions of threads like this one. And, in every case, we determine when and how long we will participate based solely on what suits us. Time like that can spoil you for the real world.

Self.   Buyers and sellers on eBay adopt a name by which they will be known. The eBay name of the woman selling the quilt I was interested in was "firewife30." Firewife30 is an identity, a self, that lives only within eBay. If she's a selfish bastard elsewhere but always acts with honor in her eBay transactions, the "elsewhere" is not a part of firewife30 that I can know about or should particularly care about. The real-world person behind firewife30 may even have other eBay identities. Perhaps she's also SexyUndies who had 132 "sexy items" for sale at eBay while firewife30 was auctioning her quilt. Unlike real-world selves, these selves are intermittent and, most important, they are written. For all we know, firewife30 started out as firewife1 and it's taken her this many drafts to craft a self that feels right to her.

Knowledge.   I began my eBay search ignorant about quilts. By browsing among the 248 quilts for sale, I inadvertently received an education. Yes, I could easily use the Web as a research tool, and at times during my quest I ran down some information—"sashing" is a border around each quilt block,[5] and a good quilter gets 10–12 stitches per inch[6]—but I learned more and learned faster by listening to the voices of the quilters on eBay. I got trained in the features to look for, what quilters consider to be boast-worthy, and what the other bidders thought was worth plunking their money down for. This was unsystematic and uncertified knowledge, but because it came wrapped in a human voice, it was richer and, in some ways, more reliable: the lively plurality of voices sometimes can and should outweigh the stentorian voice of experts.

If a simple auction at eBay is based on new assumptions about space, time, self, and knowledge, the Web is more than a place for disturbed teenagers to try out roles and more than a good place to buy cheap quilts.

———

The Web* has sent a jolt through our culture, zapping our economy, our ideas about sharing creative works, and possibly even institutions such as religion and government. Why? How do we explain the lightning charge of the Web? If it has fallen short of our initial hopes and fears about its transformational powers, why did it excite those hopes and fears in the first place? Why did this technology hit our culture like a bolt from Zeus?

Suppose—just suppose—that the Web is a new world that we're just beginning to inhabit. We're like the early European settlers in the United States, living on the edge of the forest. We don't know what's there and we don't know exactly what we need to do to find out: Do we pack mountain climbing gear, desert wear, canoes, or all three? Of course, while the settlers may not have known what the geography of the New World was going to be, they at least knew that there was a geography. The Web, on the other hand, has no geography, no landscape. It has

———

*I purposely conflate the Internet and the Web throughout this book. The distinction is very real from the technical and historical perspectives, but it isn't being observed in the public consciousness: email and home pages seem to be part of the same phenomenon even though the former is the Internet and the latter is the Web.

no distance. It has nothing natural in it. It has few rules of behavior and fewer lines of authority. Common sense doesn't hold there, and uncommon sense hasn't yet emerged. No wonder we're having trouble figuring out how to build businesses in this new land. We don't yet even know how to talk about a place that has no soil, no boundaries, no near, no far.

New worlds create new people. This has always been the case because how we live in our world is the same thing as who we are. Are we charitable? Self-centered? Cheerful? Ambitious? Pessimistic? Gregarious? Stoic? Forgiving? Each of these describes how we are engaged with our world but each can also be expressed as the way our world appears to us. If we're egotistical, the world appears to revolve around us. If we're gregarious, the world appears to be an invitation to be with others. If we're ambitious, the world appears to await our conquest. We can't characterize ourselves without simultaneously drawing a picture of how the world seems to us, and we can't describe our world without simultaneously describing the type of people we are. If we are entering a new world, then we are also becoming new people.

Obviously, we're not being recreated from the ground up. We don't talk in an affect-less voice, express curiosity about the ways of earthlings, and get an irresistible urge to mate once every seven years. But we are rewriting ourselves on the Web, hearing voices we're surprised to find coming from us, saying things we might not have expected. We're meeting people we would never have dreamed of encountering. More important, we're meeting new aspects of ourselves. We're finding out that we can be sappier, more caustic, less patient, more forgiving, angrier, funnier, more driven, less demanding, sexier, and more prudish—sometimes within a single ten-minute stretch online. We're falling into email relationships that, stretching themselves over years, imperceptibly deepen, like furrows worn into a stone hallway by the traffic of slippers. We're falling into groups that feel sometimes like parties and sometimes like battles. We're getting to know many more people in many more associations than the physics of the real world permits, and these molecules, no longer bound to the solid earth, have gained both the randomness and the freedom of the airborne. Even our notion of self as a continuous body moving through a continuous map of space and time is beginning to seem wrong on the Web.

If this is true, then for all the overheated, exaggerated, manic-depressive coverage of the Web, we'd have to conclude that the Web has not yet been hyped enough.

In 1995, when media coverage of the Web was at its most hysterical, psychologists at Carnegie Mellon University gave computers, software, and Internet access to ninety-three Pittsburgh families who had never been online before. While a significant portion of the globe was wearing out the thesaurus in the hunt for synonyms for "exciting" to describe the promise of the Web, and another portion with equal passion saw the Web as the final smut-filled convulsion of civilization, the Carnegie Mellon scientists calmly studied these families for two years, asking them questions about their patterns of usage, their outside interactions, and their mental states. In the fall of 1998, the results began to leak out: for a significant number of these families, "Internet use led to their having, on balance, less social engagement and poorer psychological well-being."[7] Not surprisingly, the study was featured on the front page of the *New York Times*.

Two years later, in the fall of 2000, another study was featured in the *New York Times*. Headlined "Who Says Surfers Are Antisocial?"—and ignoring the obvious riposte that it was the *Times* who had said it just two years earlier—the article reported that a study of 2,000 people by the University of California at Los Angeles had found that Internet users increased their contact with others, made online friends, and spent just as much time with their families as before. They were also watching 28 percent less television.[8]

The studies caused controversy individually and in comparison. Were the samples fair? Why didn't the Carnegie Mellon study use a control group? Had the Internet changed in the five years between the start of the first and the end of the second study, as suggested by one of the first study's authors?[9] But more was at stake than the quality of the science. That each of these opposing stories was front-page news exposed some of the disquiet behind the public passion for the Web. At the time the media were focused on how the Web was making twenty-five-year-old software jockeys into billionaires, how upstart companies were threatening the largest "bricks and mortar" corporations, and how investors were grumbling if they didn't make ten times their money in eighteen months. But we—the great mass of Web users—knew there was more to the story than how the money was being made and, later, lost. We knew the Web was affecting more than our bank accounts and our "shopping experience." It was changing the way we're social, for example.

The truth is that neither of these studies could really answer the question "Is the Web making us more or less social?" much less the broader question "What is the Web doing to us as social animals?" Even if we assume that both studies are paragons of the scientific method, the best they could do is answer some highly specific questions: Are Net users watching more or less television? Are we spending more or less time with our friends in the real world? These questions are only interesting, however, because they give us factual pegs on which to hang our intuitive sense that something big is happening.

We're worried, we're giddy, we're confused. If our way of being social is different on the Web, it surfaces questions that give us vertigo. For example, much of our sociality depends upon drawing the line between our private and our public lives: a friend is close if you can tell her that you're secretly quite religious, that your sex life is other than she thought, that you're not as confident as you may seem. Likewise, it's a serious transgression to ask questions more personal than we're entitled to ask; "So, how much money do you make?" and "You and your spouse doing it much?" are more likely to prevent intimacy than to foster it. Because the line between public and private is so important to us—we use words such as "embarrassment" and "humiliation" to describe what happens when the line is crossed—we generally know the rules so well that we don't have to think about them. But the Web is putting us into positions where the lines are not just blurry but have been redrawn according to a new set of rules that don't yet make sense to us. Even something as straightforward as email is catching many of us unwittingly on the wrong side of the line. For example, in October 1999, Xerox fired forty people for email abuse.[10] At the beginning of December 1999, the *New York Times* fired twenty-three employees at a Virginia payroll processing center for sending "inappropriate and offensive" email—reportedly off-color jokes. At the same time, the navy reported that it had disciplined more than five hundred employees at a Pennsylvania supply depot for sending sexually explicit email. These crackdowns on email "abuse" expose a fissure. On the one side, email is like mail—you type it in and send it to someone. On the other, email is like a conversation—you talk about whatever you want, you make jokes, you don't bother to re-read it before you send it, and you forget about it ten minutes later. So which is it? A formal letter or an informal conversation? Get it wrong, draw the line between public and private inaccurately, and you could end up being fired.[11]

Or worse. In May 2000, John Paul Denning found himself locked up in the Bellevue Hospital's ward for the mentally disturbed—his shoelaces confiscated as a precaution against suicide—because he'd written an email to an old friend in which he said, "Maybe I should stop showing people my new gun, but I'm so proud of it. Makes me feel like a real New Yorker," as well as some references to the mayhem he could commit.[12] New York University expelled Denning when they heard about this, although eventually a board of inquiry readmitted him when he was able to show that the email was simply dark humor sent to a close friend.

The problems we have finding the new lines between the public and the private are part of the more general problem of understanding how to coordinate the two worlds, one real and one virtual. Consider Tom Alciere, elected to the New Hampshire state legislature in November 2000.[13] The barrier was low: it costs $2 to register as a candidate, and the position pays a lordly $100 a year ... plus free passage through state highway tollbooths. A circuit-board inspector for a local electronics company, Alciere ran as a Republican in a heavily Democratic ward, although in his six previous bids at public office he had run variously as a Democrat and as a Libertarian. The four-way race received almost no coverage, and Alciere squeaked in with a fifty-five-vote margin, possibly because his name was listed first on the ballot. Only a couple of weeks after he was sworn in did anyone notice that The Honorable Tom Alciere had a home page that called for eliminating mandatory school attendance and removing the age restrictions on drinking. On a site devoted to the topic of suicide, Alciere weighed in with his suggestion that one way to get "sweet revenge against the government for making everybody's life miserable ... is to waste as many cops as possible before you die." Turning to practical considerations, he recommended driving a truck into the crowd at a police officer's funeral. When the legislator resigned thirty-six days later, he sent an email that explained how he had managed to get himself elected: "Well, nobody asked me if I liked cops, or supported the drug laws, etc." Alciere told the truth about himself in a globally public forum. He did nothing to hide his views. It's quite likely that the voters in his district in New Hampshire have learned a lesson: what counts as "the public sphere" has changed. It now includes the Web. We're just not sure how.

———

You could look at these examples as anomalies—a quiet teenager who makes cruel threats on the Web; scores of workers who are fired for saying in email only what they would have said in person; and a fringe candidate who's blunt about his out-rageous views on the Web without any effect on his campaign. But just about everywhere we turn, the Web upsets our expec-tations. Sharing copyrighted music files seemed perfectly proper to 70 million Napster users. Companies that compete form cooperative Net marketplaces. Pornography that you once had to go to Sweden to find you can't now avoid. The best sources of information about products are online customer forums, not the companies that create the products. Children play ultra-violent online games with the innocence of a game of tag. Hundreds of millions of people are building a transnational infrastructure without guidance, assistance, or permission. So many things don't make sense on the Web that we're suffering from Anomaly Fatigue.

Perhaps it's just as well, for focusing on anomalies can be a way of denying the disturbing nature of what passes for normal. Just as arguments about, say, abortion are the least likely to lead to an understanding of the nature of morality—far better to watch how we humans accomplish our ordinary acts of decency—so, too, if we want to understand what the Web is doing to something as basic as our social natures, we need to look at our everyday experiences of the Web. Besides, does any-one really want to keep on arguing about Napster?

So let's not pound our heads against the anomalies. We can learn more by looking at something perfectly ordinary on the Web. For example, if we want to study the Web's effect on our sociality, we could look at "weblogs," or online journals, for there you can see the redrawing of the line between public and private. In 2000, a few sites began offering tools that made it so easy to create and maintain a weblog that all you had to do was type in the content. As a result, an estimated 100,000 weblogs exist now, although the actual number is unknowable.

Let's take a random example. Someone named .Zannah (yes, the leading dot, the visual equivalent of a pierced tongue, is part of her Web identity) has a weblog titled "/usr/bin/girl" (the technoid-sounding name refers to standard Unix directories.)[14] The page's main serving consists of frequent write-ups about Web sites that .Zannah finds interesting:

> This site [www.compugarg.com] sells Computer Gargoyles, to watch over you as you surf the 'net. . . .

> Taco Joe's graphics are silly at best, which led me to believe that I wouldn't like this game. However, upon giving it a chance, I found myself somewhat enthralled with the taco making, roach squashing business. . . .

> Open Cola, the world's first open source cola. I have no idea how it tastes, but I'm fairly amused at the idea of an open-source food or drink. . . .

Good information that might help a hapless browser find some useful sites. But .Zannah isn't merely conveying information. In the left-hand margin, .Zannah lifts her veil, providing lists of what matters to her, including "recently acquired items" ("blue vinyl pants, rhinestone chain, hair toys, replicant shirt, glowsticks . . .") and a list that's harder to categorize:

> mixellanea randomosity:
> I am 65.465% insane.
> I'm 42% bitchy.
> I'm an idealist.
> I'm also sensitive.

My geek quotient is 63.
I'm a pink grapefruit.
I'm right between pessimism & optimism.

If you follow the links, you find that these are the results of various sarcastic quizzes around the Web. Despite—or is it because of?—the irony and sarcasm, the reader begins to get a sense of this young woman.

Then, in one corner, there's a link to a personal home page, a second place for .Zannah to expose herself to the public in highly controlled ways.[15] The weblog page is updated more frequently than her home page, but the two pages also differ in the types of disclosures they publish. It's almost as if they were the views two different friends might have of her, each site drawing the line between the public and the private differently. The home page doesn't feel quite as free; it appears to be tied more closely to her offline self—for example, she discloses her physical location—although the differences are more in tone than content. In the upper left corner of her home page, there's a picture of her. She looks as if she's in her early twenties. Head bent down, black hair falling in parentheses past her face, her eyes looking up to make direct contact. An appealing, knowing face. But, if you leave your mouse cursor over the face for more than a few seconds, up pops a caption. It reads: "[just some random chick]." So, is the photograph of .Zannah or is it truly just a random photo? Her webcam is off right now, but the last image it recorded is there. The random chick is .Zannah all right. The caption is just some misdirection. Probably.

What's going on here? Personal revelations, but enough irony to make sure we don't trust them too much. A name that begins with punctuation, a carefully constructed set of sarcastic lists that tell us about herself, and a clue that what we're reading is a mix of self-revelation and self-invention. Is she being sociable on the Web? She is certainly playing in public with others. But how can we make sense of the evidence about whether the Web is making us less social if we're not certain what it means to be social in this new world?

.Zannah is no Michael Ian Campbell; she is not channeling John Malkovich and making idle threats to a student recently terrorized in a school shooting. She's not insane and she's not an anomaly. For all her oddness, her quirkiness, her postmodern irony, .Zannah is the norm of the Web. She is what's ordinary. The real problem we face with the Web is not understanding the anomalies but facing how deeply weird the ordinary is.

────────

When I met Mike O'Dell, he was chief scientist at UUnet, one of the main providers of the Internet "backbone," the wires and routers that in one sense are the Internet. We were at the first meeting of a small conference in intensely quaint Woods Hole, Massachusetts. O'Dell dominated the meeting. Although the conference was intended to bring together hard-nosed engineers and soft-hearted social commentators, O'Dell was so adept at using facts like brass knuckles and slapping us softies down with a swipe of his hand that we thought a second and a third time before venturing into the conversational arena. There seemed to be nothing he didn't know. When I went home and told my wife about the weekend, I mainly described how smart and intimidating I found O'Dell. Yet, within a few months, he and I had become good friends through email. It's a better medium for us because neither of us is tempted to show off by being gratuitously right in public.

Almost a year after Big Hook, I wrote to Mike and asked him to take a guess at how much data at any one moment is in the wires that compose the Internet. He responded almost immediately. Based on guesstimates of the total mileage of wires carrying Net traffic and the average speed with which bits are moved through those wires, Mike estimated that at any one moment, between five and ten gigabytes of information are in the wires. A gigabyte is 1,073,741,824 bytes (2 to the 30th power)—call it an even billion—enough to encode about 3,000 books of average length. Thus, at any moment, the equivalent of a small library, 15,000 to 30,000 books, is in transit over the Internet. Just one wire going across the United States, O'Dell estimates, carries about 3 megabytes of information. If we consider not merely the text but all the other information that's included in a high-quality electronic book—information about page layout and fonts, for example—if an e-book of *Hamlet* started in Boston, Fortinbras would be ringing down the curtain just fifteen miles short of Akron, Ohio.[16]

Books stretched to the height of one bit and strung between telephone polls make for an arresting image, especially if one keeps in mind that these libraries are rushing through the wires at the speed of light, pulsing at intervals on the order of one ten-billionth of a second. O'Dell calls his calculation the number of "bytes in flight," a lovely phrase. Even though this view of the Internet isn't useful to most of us, it claims our attention. So do many views that have been put forward: the Web as technological marvel, as the millionaire-maker, as the modern Gold Rush, as the new economy that will raise all boats and sink old rules.

Then the weekly magazines arrive and the lead stories are about the anomaly of the week: the music our kids are downloading without paying for it when they wouldn't dream of shoplifting it; the bankrupt companies selling their lists of customers to creditors even though the customers thought they'd been assured of privacy; the juicy rumors being circulated by people who are sober and careful about what they say in the real world.

All these views of the Web are true enough and fair enough. But if we're to make any progress in understanding the Web's effect on us—including but certainly not limited to the question "Is the Web making us more or less social?"—we need something more than Yet Another View. We need a way to address this question and a thousand others, but we seem to lack the basic stance. We have a hundred ways of considering the Web, from bytes in flight to technological infrastructure to economic playing field to entertainment medium to global conversation to a wanker's paradise. But none seems adequate to the task. Our ways of thinking about the Web, even ones as evocative as Mike's bytes in flight, have tended to make the Web too small to account for the effect it's having.

————

If we were to investigate a "big idea" such as democracy, we would look at how its introduction in the eighteenth century affected a suite of related terms basic to our understanding of ourselves in a world of others: citizen, rights, duties, equality, justice, nation, government, authority, legitimacy, law, morality, human nature. In a parallel fashion, as we've looked at just one sample question about the Web—does it make us more or less social?—we've found ourselves brought to consider terms as basic as self, society, friendship, knowledge, morality, authority, private, and public. It is a measure of the importance of the Web that to understand it we find ourselves rethinking bedrock notions of our culture.

But democracy had such a powerful effect, overturning governments and changing the social order, only because it occurred within an oppressive culture of monarchy and aristocracy. Who you were depended on who you were born as, and clearly not everyone was born equal. Democracy was an explosive idea only because this context of inequality pressed so hard against it. The Web's power likewise comes from the pressure of the atmosphere into which it was born. Just as the opposite of democracy was aristocracy, the opposite of the virtual world of the Web is the real world. The Web explodes out with precisely the same force with which the real world pushes in.

It's easy to see what was so oppressive about aristocracy and all that went with it, but what's so oppressive about the real world? Yes, having to travel distances to get where we're going is a bother, but the Web's distancelessness isn't enough to explain the force with which the Web has hit us. After all, telephones and faxes also eliminate distance. Something more has to be going on.

A few years ago, I listened to a woman calling in to a legal expert on a radio talk show. Her basement apartment had taken in a few feet of water in a flood. She didn't have insurance and the landlord's insurance didn't cover the damage. The legal expert explained that the caller was out of luck. Floods happen. The caller was outraged. Who was going to replace her appliances and furniture, not to mention the keepsakes now ruined forever? This was an injustice! I listened with sympathy, for I had been through a flood many years ago, but I also listened with amazement. A bad thing had happened to this woman, so she expected compensation to make it all better. It was as if the world had not lived up to its side of a contract.

Her demand was unreasonable, but her premises, I believe, are widely shared in our culture. Bad things aren't part of "the deal." There isn't a problem we don't assume we will solve eventually. Cancer will soon be cured. AIDS is on the run. We'll figure out a way to mend the hole in the ozone layer and to reverse global warming. Terrorism will be rooted out. We just need to marshal the facts and manage the project. The dinosaurs could only look up in dismay as the asteroid slammed towards them, but we'll organize an international project, preferably with Bruce Willis at the helm, and we'll nuke that sucker back to the Stone Age. We are the masters of our fate. We can manage our way out of any problem.*

The building of the Hoover Dam is perhaps the emblematic example of the power of traditional management. The six companies responsible for the project had to construct a city in the desert to house 5,000 workers, complete with a water and sewer system, a city hall, laundries, schools, police and fire departments, and a hospital. They had to build a 222-mile extension of the power system to bring electricity to the site. They spent seven months building a 22.7-mile railroad and a 400-car switchyard. To deliver materials, they built a cableway 1,580 feet long. Even the simplest aspects of the dam's construction

---

*As I write this, the United States is reeling from the attack on the World Trade Center and the Pentagon. This has shaken our sense of mastery with results that cannot yet be predicted.

often turned out to be hideously complex, requiring ingenious solutions. For example, moving pipes a mile and a half from their fabrication plant required building specially designed 16-wheeled, 38-foot-long trailers with tractors in the rear devoted simply to braking, and two-tier cars to bring the pipes to their final destination.[17] The Hoover Dam is a masterpiece of management as well as of engineering.

The Web, however, is teaching us a different lesson about management. Consider the Web as a construction project. It's the most complex network ever created. It is by many orders of magnitude the largest collection of human writings and works in history. It is far more robust than networks far smaller, yet it was created without managers. In fact, it succeeded only because its designers made the conscious decision to build a network that would require no central control. You don't need anyone's permission to join in, to post whatever you want, to read whatever others have posted. The Web is profoundly unmanaged, and that is crucial to its success. It takes traditional command and control structures and busts them up into many small pieces that then loosely join themselves—and that, too, is crucial to its success.

As a result, the Web is a mess, as organized as an orgy. It consists of voices proclaiming whatever they think is worth saying, trying on stances, experimenting with extremes, being wrong in public, making fun of what they hold sacred in their day jobs, linking themselves into permanent coalitions and drive-by arguments, savoring the rush you feel when you realize you don't have to be the way you've been.

The Web has driven through the plate glass window of traditional management. Because every surprise is an affront to the managed world—not anticipating market trends or the actions of competitors can give a management team the opportunity to "pursue other interests"—we agree to play by the rules so that we won't surprise anyone and no one will surprise us. We become professionals by adhering to a code of conduct that has us all sounding the same. We manage our time into neat segments of work, home, recreation, sleep. We focus on the facts because that's how we get predictability. We aim for an objectivity that suppresses individual viewpoints and passion.

But we pay a price psychologically and sociologically for repressing our differences and it goes beyond psychology. It has to do with the fundamentals of our world. Our real-world view of *space* says that it consists of homogenous measurable distances laid across an arbitrary geography indifferent to human needs; the Web's geography, on the other hand, consists of links among pages each representing a spring of human interest. Real-world *time* consists of ticking clocks and the relentless schedules they enable; on the Web, time runs as intertwining threads and stories. In the real world, *perfection* is held as an ideal we humans always disappoint; on the Web, perfection just gets in the way. In the real world, *social groups* become more impersonal as they get larger; on the Web, individuals retain their faces no matter what the size of the group—even in the "faceless mass" of the public. In the real world, we have thinned our knowledge down to a flavorless stream of verifiable facts; on the Web, knowledge is fat with stories and voice. Our "realistic" view of *matter* says that it's the stuff that exists independent of us, and as such it is essentially apart from whatever meanings we cast over it like shadows; the matter of the Web, on the other hand, consists of pages that we've built, full of intention and meaning. In the real world, to be *moral* means we follow a set of principles; while on the Web, resorting to principles looks like prissiness, and authenticity, empathy, and enthusiasm instead guide our interactions.

If the Web is changing bedrock concepts such as space, time, perfection, social interaction, knowledge, matter, and morality—each a chapter of this book—no wonder we're so damn confused. That's as it should be. A new world is opening up, a world that we create as we explore it. .Zannah is inventing it, Michael Ian Campbell is abusing it, and every person browsing and posting is setting bytes in flight that shape this new world. Space, time, perfection, social interaction, knowledge, matter, and morality—this is the vocabulary of the Web, not the bits and the bytes, the dot-coms and not-coms, the e-this and B2That. The Web is a world we've made for one another. It can be understood only within a web of ideas that includes our culture's foundational thoughts, with human spirit lingering at every joining point.

chapter two

SPACE

ON BILL CHESWICK'S HOME PAGE you'll find a bit of visual leg-erdemain, the "McCollough Effect."[1] It's not quite an optical illusion, although at first it seems like one—you stare at some colored bars and then "see" a nimbus of purple around vertical black stripes. But, unlike an optical illusion, the effect lasts for days, giving you the unsettling feeling that looking at the bars has rewired your brain. If you want to visit Bill's home page to try this out, he'll tell you to type "cheswick" into the address box at the top of your browser, as if it were built with his address specially encoded in it.[2] In reality, he's relying on the fact that some browsers automatically fill in the "www." before and ".com" after a single word. Ches (as he likes to be called) isn't really trying to trick you; he's just playing with the seam where technology and magic meet.

You need this sense of play to be an Internet security guru. That was Ches's role at Bell Labs in Murray Hill, New Jersey, where they were registering a "mere" three patents a day when I met with him. If your job is to outthink hackers, you need to understand the Net at several levels at once: its hardware, the protocols by which computers establish communication, the languages computers speak, and the applications users run that access the inner workings of the computer and thus present a vulnerable belly. You also need a sense of playfulness that will let you anticipate your nemesis' quirks of genius. These qualities of vision are characteristic of people who love maps, for maps show an overview and details all at once. So perhaps it should have been no surprise when Ches unrolled a large piece of paper printed on an oversized printer, introducing it as a distraction from our real reason for meeting. Our work had turned into play.

It took both of us to hold the scrolled paper open while Ches admired his handiwork (created with his coworker, Hal Burch). It looked like a particularly chaotic set of fireworks, starbursts in a hundred colors, overlapping and messy. Or perhaps it was more like a roomful of mutant spider plants. It was an arresting image but it told me nothing.

"This," said Ches, "is a map of the Internet."

It was, to be more precise, a map of the hardware of the Net, the routers that move the packets of information requested whenever a user clicks on a hyperlink. As Ches put it, it showed "the tin cans and string" of the Net. His voice became even more animated as he pointed out cluttered areas representing subsurface Internet backbone providers that few users have heard of.

It's a view that corresponds to nothing that users ever see, like a multilayer map of a city. The top layer shows the city streets and buildings, the tourist attractions starred. The next layer shows the subway system, perhaps in a stylized manner to make it more readable. The bottom layer shows the gas, water, sewage, and electrical conduits, arranged to show how they connect, not how they relate to the top level of the map. This bottom layer corresponds to Ches's map. It's useful to those who can interpret it—the colors show clusters of IP addresses and thus areas of potential blockages—but this is not a map of a space any more than it is a map of a family tree. It's useful and interesting precisely because it shows the Net organized by clusters of connections, space freed of geography.[3]

"This is a map of the Web," says Tim Bray, on the other edge of the continent, pointing at a computer screen that shows, unexpectedly, a map of Antarctica.

Tim is one of the Web pioneers. Although one can mark the beginning of the Web with Tim Berners-Lee's invention of HTML, the language of Web pages, there is a different history to be written as well, one that focuses on two decades of thought about the business problems posed by documents. Documents are stunningly deep artifacts. Just about all business information worth knowing is expressed in them. Yet, once you put an idea into a business plan, a memo, an invoice, or a white paper, there's no easy way to find it, extract it, and reuse it. Tim Bray was one of the leaders in the effort to solve these problems, focusing on finding information in documents. When the Web hit the world, Tim was able to take the software he'd written and use it to create one of the very first Web search sites. In fact, if you did a search on the contents of Yahoo back in the early days, you were using Tim's work. Given his long interest in helping people navigate through masses of pages, it's not surprising that his start-up is centered on mapping webs—it's the same set of problems, although this particular solution uses pictures to navigate through the Web's words.[4]

Tim and I are looking straight down at what started its life as a satellite image of the frozen continent. We type in what we're looking for—vegetarian recipes—and the site returns a list of topics, such as Home/Recipes/Vegetarian and Home/Recipes/World_Cuisine/Eastern_Asian/Chinese/Vegetarian, representing the branches of a broad outline of topics that is similar to what you see at Yahoo. In this case, the outline of available sites is built by the Open Directory Project, a volunteer group of tens of thousands of people who suggest sites that ought to be included in the listing. We decide to visit one of the topics, and pick a view that is relatively close to the ground; the higher up you are, the closer you are to the start of the outline and the more general the topic is. The map of Antarctica is populated with labels showing the category we're looking for as well as neighboring categories. We click to drop down a level until we're looking at markers indicating the Web sites themselves. Sites are represented by three concentric rings like a bull's-eye target. The thickness of the black outer ring tells you how many links the page has; the thickness of the blue ring tells you how many other pages link to it; and the thickness of the inner white circle tells you how many pages are on the site. Thus, a quick scan tells you a lot about the richness and popularity of each site. We click on one with lots of links out and in, and find ourselves on a Web site devoted to vegetarian cooking.

Just when I think we're done, Tim clicks on a button and now we're not hovering above Antarctica but have dropped to ground level. The circles seen from above now look like buildings, their appearance designed to convey information about the site. By using the mouse and arrow keys, we can move through the "streets," buildings growing larger as they approach. Tim presses the "Page Up" key and now we're flying. Beneath us are clusters of sites on related topics, little villages of recipes and hamlets of vegetarian information. Tim clicks on one and the site it represents opens up in a separate browser window. We come back, speed past some Chinese recipes and land in a tiny town of vegetarian lasagna recipes.

Map or video game? Does it matter? On the Web, information can be its own reward.

Ches's map and Tim's map are worlds apart. Ches's shows the Internet, the global network that predates and enables the Web; Tim's shows the Web. Ches's shows hardware; Tim's shows Web sites, which ultimately are software. Ches's clusters are based on their physical connections; Tim's clusters are based on guesses about similarity of topic. Ches's shows relationships that help our understanding; Tim's helps us navigate. And both maps are very different from maps of the earth. Ches and Tim could change their plotting algorithms and their "land masses" would radically shift. And although both maps are graphical, Tim's Web maps are unlike any maps of the earth ever created since the Egyptians first asked what the world might look like to a high-flying bird: clicking on Tim's map takes you to the place you touched. In the real world, that happens only in dreams involving genies and lanterns.

Yet, the real mystery is this: Why does it make any sense at all to create maps of a world that is so profoundly nonspatial? Why does the Web—accessed through a computer that shows us a 2-D screen of colored bits—seem so resolutely spatial when it's not spatial at all?

We carry with us two distinct conceptions of space. On the one hand, there's the space we walk around in; this is filled with tangible things such as houses, trees, and bicycles. On the other hand, there's the space we measure with odometers, yardsticks, and surveying-equipment rulers. These two spaces, lived space and measured space, are quite distinct. Lived space is different everywhere we look. Except for a moonless night in a flat, featureless desert, or the blackness of a sensory deprivation booth, during every waking moment of every day we are surrounded by differentiated sensations. Actually, that's not accurate. We're not surrounded by sensations but by *stuff*—the things of our world, each with some meaning to us. Our space is full of opportunities, obstacles, and dangers, or what the psychologist James Gibson called *affordances* (e.g., the chair affords us the possibility of sitting) and the philosopher Martin Heidegger called the ready-to-hand.[5] This lived space is the opposite of measured space composed of uniform segments like the grid on a map.

We invented measured space because it's useful. And we did so a long time ago; just consider the ancient origins of the term *foot*. But thanks to seventeenth-century thinkers such as Sir

Isaac Newton and René Descartes, we took measured space one step further and began to visualize a universal, three-dimensional gridwork within which anything can be precisely located. We have so abstracted this grid that we believe that the entire universe fits snugly inside it. But the difference between knowing that we can, when required, measure something and believing that space consists of uniform, measured distances is vast. Because we measure things to make them fit, we pay close attention to the things we measure. But the grid is supposedly always there, independent of the things in it. The grid, considered in itself, turns our attention away from the stuff of our world. Nevertheless, it has become the very definition of space according to our "default philosophy," the set of beliefs about our world that we hold so deeply that it feels like common sense.

If the Web is a space, it's incapable of supporting a gridwork. There can't be an overlay of equally distant points because the Web is a space without distance, at least not in any usual sense. Yes, you could play with Ches's map of the Net until the router placements correspond to their placement on the earth, and then you could overlay a grid on top of that. But that would be a map of where the Web's hardware is housed. That might be useful; it could remind you to be careful when digging up your backyard, for example, but it wouldn't be a map of the Web. To achieve this grid, we've had to reduce the Web to a set of computers. But that's precisely what's not interesting about it. The Web space is composed of pages and sites that are located relative to one another but not in an abstract spatial grid. The Web is a special kind of space.

What type? Let's try a thought experiment. Imagine you're an English professor doing research on *Moby Dick*. You do most of your work in the huge university library, where you have a carrel with a large writing surface and surprisingly large storage cabinets. As you begin your research, you want to get the lay of the land, so you browse the vast literature about Melville's classic by picking a starting point and being guided by the footnotes and bibliographies of the books you're reading. So you request your first book from the stacks. Every faculty member has his or her own underpaid graduate student. Yours is named Bob. All you have to do is tap your finger on the reference and the ever-alert Bob runs to the stacks to retrieve it for you.

You read along. You find an interesting footnote that refers to another book. You tap. Up comes Bob with the book. You make notes, and you find some pertinent references in the bibliography of the second book. Down goes Bob as he loads your requested books on a cart and delivers them to you. More footnotes, more bibliographies, more trips into the stacks by Bob. After a couple of weeks, you're at book #500; you seem to have just about all the relevant books at hand and carefully organized in the carrel so that you can find the one you need in only a few seconds. Bob takes a well-earned nap.

Now imagine that you are doing the same research but on the Web. The same 500 books are all online. Their footnotes and bibliographic references are all hyperlinked. You have a touch screen, so all you have to do is press on the reference to activate the hyperlink; this action is just like what you had to do with the real books in your carrel. And, to keep the analogy, let's say that because the connection is bad, the hyperlinks work about as quickly as Bob (who, I may not have mentioned, is an Olympic roller skater). After a couple of weeks, you've browsed through the same 500 books.

Now, we've constructed two situations, one hugely artificial, the other fairly realistic. In both cases, you're reading documents, touching links, and then reading the documents the links point to. The only difference is that in one case the documents are printed on paper and in the other they're sprayed across glass. Despite the similarities, our *experience* of these two situations will be quite different. Consider the language we'll use. In the first case, we'll *take* a book *from* the shelf, find a link, *get* another book and *put* the first one *back*. In the physical carrel, I'm the still center of the universe. I cause things to be brought to me and to be taken away when I have finished with them. Now consider the language we use to talk about the Web experience: we *go to* a *site*, we *browse,* we *surf,* we find a link and we *go* to it. When we're done, we *leave* the site. The carrel is a place where we sit; the Web is a space through which we travel.

So our very language tells us. And it's not just a few casual words that happen to use spatial imagery. The economy of the Web is being built around the idea that it's a space. We're building "stores," worrying about the impact of Web "malls," running ads to bring users "in," making our sites "sticky" to keep users from "leaving," providing aids so that users can "navigate." Space isn't a mere metaphor. The rhetoric and semantics of the Web are those of space. More important, our *experience* of the Web is fundamentally spatial.

In our thought experiment, the two cases are identical except that one of them delivers documents digitally over the Web. It seems that there's something about the Web itself that turns the book experience into a spatial one.

Part of it has to do, oddly, with the fact that the Web is a series of documents. Documents—pages—are the stuff of the

Web. This is a good thing, for we are all intimately acquainted with the operating instructions for documents, the most complex presentations of information that humans deal with. From the time we sit on our parent's lap as he or she reads picture books to us, we are taught the information structures behind documents, starting with pages and pictures with captions. By the time we're eight or so, we can parse a newspaper, understanding which elements are headlines, stories, headers, footers, subheads, and ads. The information structures of newspapers are amazingly complex, but we navigate them as if we were born to the job.

Without documents, the Web would be as boring as the Internet from which it sprang. We'd be scrolling through character-based screens of information without the benefits to the eye and mind of multiple fonts and careful layout. But, because sites are documents, we've already been trained to parse them. Because we're used to magazines, we immediately grasp the purpose of the left-hand sidebar used by many sites. Because we're used to books, we understand the purpose of a site's table of contents. Because we're used to reports, we make sense of information presented in table form. We've been well trained.

But Web documents are weird. This is to be expected given the odd history of the concept of the document. Sometimes when I give talks, I play a game called "Am I a Document?" I show the audience a photo of a book and ask them if it's a document. Everyone of course says yes. Next, airplane tickets? Definitely. But how about a candy wrapper with a list of ingredients and nutritional information? Yes, probably. The back of a cereal box? Yeah, since we read it at breakfast, why not? A T-shirt with a slogan on it? Half the people say no, until I zoom in on the label and point out the washing directions—the shirt's instruction manual. A musical score is definitely a document, but how about a recording of it being performed? Sky writing? Smoke signals? A coded knock on a door signaling that I'm a friend? A burning bush? Amazingly, there's always at least one person who says yes to each of these. The concept of the document has become elastic almost to the point of meaningless-ness.[6]

Before computers, we knew exactly what documents were. And outside the world of computing, we're quite clear about them. Documents are a special class of things with writing on them, including passports, leases, contracts, an original copy of the United States Constitution, and Napoleon's hand-drawn map of Waterloo. To be a document, it has to play a special role in our legal or historical systems such that a copy simply won't do.

How did such a clear and specialized concept get so confused? In the 1970s, the makers of word processing systems were looking for a word that would distinguish their files from those of other applications. They needed a term of sufficient generality to include everything one could write with their software, and, surprisingly, there was no such term in our language; the closest is perhaps "writings," and that doesn't work very well in the singular. So the word processors took over the term *document,* and if you are old enough to have been in on the first round of personal computers, you may remember being struck by how out of place the term seemed.

But then word processors became more powerful and flexible. The files they create can now include images, sounds, and movies. And it's not just word processors that create these types of files. Your spreadsheet, your database, your Web page editor can all do the same things. The so-called document was stretched to include just about everything you can make visible with a computer program. Since the stretching happened without plan or definition, the term has become vague and without clear borders. That's why we run into difficulty when we try to define a computer document or even figure out whether my tie, as a fashion statement, might conceivably count as a document.

As a result, the word *document* has opposite meanings inside and outside the computing world. Outside, documents are unique originals; inside the world of computers, they are perfectly copy-able. Outside, documents are high-value; inside, everything from a will to a grocery list is a document. Outside, documents are unchanging; inside, documents are there to be changed. Outside, documents are an unusual class of writings; inside, there's nothing more common than a document.

But it's a good thing that computers have broken the spine of this erstwhile well-defined concept. It has allowed computing environments, including the Web, to take advantage of the expertise we've developed in understanding complex documents and to extend and stretch the concept in ways the real world didn't and couldn't. For example, because traditional documents have accustomed us to footnotes and other pointers, we were able to comprehend hyperlinks without a hiccough.

But some of the traditional ideas concerning documents don't transfer nearly as easily, including the basic document publishing model. When we buy a physical book in a book-store, we don't expect it to be the original. In fact, we don't know quite what the original would be. The first copy printed? The author's handwritten pages? On the Web, on the other hand, matters are considerably more confusing. For example, in June 2000, hackers vandalized the Nike site, www.nike.com. They put up a political statement and directed traffic to a site where people could get information about protesting the World Trade Organization. Suppose the Web didn't exist and the hackers wanted to vandalize Nike's marketing materials. Vandalizing all the advertisements Nike was placing in magazines would have taken thousands of dedicated operatives thumbing through millions of magazines, writing their slogans over and over and over. The paper documents are all copies, although of an original that we can't quite identify. When, on the other hand, we look at the page at www.nike.com, we feel as if we're looking at the one and only. Vandalizing www.nike.com is more like vandalizing the Nike building than its marketing literature.

And this is perhaps the most significant change the Web brings to the world of documents: the Web has created a weird amalgam of documents and buildings. With normal paper documents, we read them, file them, throw them out, or send them to someone else. We do not *go* to them. We don't *visit* them. Web documents are different. They're places on the Web. We go to them as we might go to the Washington Monument or the old Endicott Building. They're there, we're here, and if we want to see them, we've got to travel.

They're *there.* With this phrase, space—or something like it—has entered the picture.

———

The odd thing is that, of course, we're not really going any place, and we know it. When we click on a link, a message is sent to the server that houses the page we want and a copy of the page is transmitted to us. If the page has lots of graphics or if the Net has indigestion, it can take a long time. We sit there watching the "Waiting" symbol in our browser and mutter under our breath. So we do in some sense know that we're dealing with copies that are being delivered—slowly—to our computers. Yet the spatial sense persists.

Perhaps this isn't so far removed from ordinary perception. We see the Washington Monument in the distance. It's there and we're here. Yet, if you were to sit us down and remind us of the physics we took in high school, we'd tell you that what we're seeing is light that's bounced off of the Monument and has arrived in our eyeballs. Nevertheless, we have the irreducible sense of seeing the original. And the same is true on the Web: we are downloading a copy, yet we feel we're seeing the original.

In the final analysis, we seem to have a choice of metaphors that are equally suited to the task. We could think of the Web as a giant photocopier that delivers copies of sites. We could think of it as a medium through which we see sites. We could think of it as a library from which we request copies. But we don't. We experience the Web as a web: a set of nodes that are linked one to another, creating a space through which we travel.

———————

There is a tie to the physical earth that helps give the Web its spatial sense. As we go to one document site after another, we have the sense that the authors of these pages are somewhere else on the planet. Sometimes we have a good sense of where— for example, if you're at the home page of Peoria Toyota

(www.peoriatoyota.com) or the Bermuda Department of
Tourism (www.bermudatourism.com)—but often we don't
have the slightest idea. But we know the authors of Web pages
are far flung around the globe. We probably also have a vague
idea that the Web servers that serve up the pages are themselves
geographically distributed. This vague connection to the earth
makes it easier for us to see the Web as a global space through
which we can move.

And, as we go from page to page, we also know that the
pages were put there for all to see. They are public. Documents
are, after all, a way people communicate. This gives us the sense
that the Web is an objective space that is bigger than any one of
us. This, too, enables our perception of the Web as a space.

———

The Web is a space, but it's different from normal space. If you
don't allow for the Web's transformation of space, you can get
some unexpected results. For example, if the Web is spatial, we
should be able to create a representation of it as 3-D space that
enables us to move around using the arrow keys on our keyboard. Indeed, several chat rooms take this approach, as does
Tim Bray's Antarctica map. Normally, in a chat you and several
other people who are online at the same time type messages at
one another that appear in a scrolling window replicated on
each person's computer desktop. In a 3-D chat room, each person is represented by a graphic of his or her own choosing,
ranging from a simple drawing of a person to fanciful animals,
monsters, and objects. These graphics, or avatars, wander
through a set of 3-D corridors and rooms. You see other
avatars, typically with speech balloons over their heads report-

ing what they're saying. If you want to join in, you just start typing.

But moving a chat into a 3-D Web space changes the nature of the chat. For example, Michael Heim, a philosopher and the author of several important books on the philosophical impact of computer and Net technology, teaches 3-D design at the Art Center College of Design in Pasadena, California.[7] He regularly runs cyber classes in which students meet via avatars online in a 3-D space. During one of Mike's lectures, I participated as a student.[8]

The 3-D world was populated with structures assembled by the students at the Art Center from a palette of basic shapes and textures, creating buildings, gardens, even free-floating cloud-like forms. The shapes had different textures, from metallic sheens to thatches. Some shimmered. Some played music as you approached. Buzzing around Michael were little cartoony characters of low resolution (i.e., made up of relatively few dots), representing each of us. I was the default avatar, a cross between a stick figure and a manikin; Michael's avatar was a plankton that looked like a pillow with four legs. To my side, one of the more practiced participants had adopted her own avatar, a gracefully dancing set of curved lines. A bird hovered, a colorful bug flitted. Certainly there must be some psychological significance to the choice of avatars, but it's as hard to read as the choice of hats—did you put on the pith helmet because you're feeling adventurous or ridiculous?

Michael began the tour by giving us some instructions. His words appeared in a comic-book balloon near his head. Using the arrow keys, we moved our avatars around and watched ourselves move through space, far from the usual earthbound experience.

The experience was different in other ways as well. For example, we could fly at will or hyperjump from one spot to another without having to cover the distance in between. And there was one more difference that may not at first seem connected to the nature of the virtual space we were in: the silly, back-of-the-classroom chatter engaged in by teenagers who have a substitute teacher for a day surfaced quite explicitly. As Michael made his points, the students kept up a constant stream of remarks about what he was saying. Some cheered him on with comments like, "That's so true!" or "The same thing happened to me . . ." with an elaboration. Others made wisecracks, some at Michael's expense, but none mean; clearly the group liked him. Side discussions broke out and drove to new points of interest or silliness. We could "whisper" asides to another person without the rest of the group knowing. The lag time after a comment was typed meant that comments often arrived after a new, unrelated comment showed up, resulting in an agreeable jumble of ideas, responses tripping over one another in an unassembled chaos.

This type of chatter wouldn't have occurred during one of Michael's classes in the real world space. We would have sat relatively quietly, not interrupting and staying on a single thread until it was done. It would not have been nearly as chaotic and digressive. If we wanted to talk while someone else was talking, we would have stifled ourselves, or, if not, we would have whispered. But online, what would have been rude in the real world turned into a valuable ingredient of the discussion itself. We were making public what would have been private in the space of the real world. And because Web space lets many things happen at the same time in the same place, we were all talking at once, connecting to various threads of conversation as they emerged.

Weird things happen in a weird space. And there are other ways the spatial analogies don't hold—which can cause problems if the differences go unthought. For example, we think of a typical ecommerce site as a store, not as a catalog, because we're comfortable with documents-as-buildings on the Web. But where do the analogies end? Supposedly, the item in a real-world grocery found in the most shopping carts is, surprisingly, bananas. So, many real-world groceries put the bananas at the back of the store to force you to traverse the aisles in hopes that you'll be tempted into doing some impulse shopping on the way to the bananas. But this would be precisely the wrong strategy for a Web store. If you force users to click many times to get to what they're looking for, they will remember that they're only one click away from your competition. We don't mind walking down the real-world aisle to get the bananas because real-world space requires some things to be further away than others. But because the Web's peculiar type of space can put everything we need within equally distanceless reach, if we think a site is making itself inconvenient on purpose, we don't get the bananas . . . we get annoyed.

But the most significant difference between real-world space and Web space has to do with the relationship of space to the things in it. Real-world space is a preexisting container in which the things of the world exist. Web space is created by the things in it. For example, the territory that Michael Heim had us visit wasn't an empty plot of Web until people built their creations; in creating the buildings, they were creating the space Michael was showing off. In Web space, no expanse of empty space gets diminished every time someone stakes a new plot on which to build a house, as it would in the real world. Web space is infinite in that it can't be used up, but it's not infinitely big. It's not a container waiting to be filled; it is more like a book that's being written.

That Web space is not a container is a point often missed in media discussions about mega mergers such as that of America Online and Time-Warner. The columnists and talking heads get in a fluster, worried that these new, giant entities will crowd out the smaller sites, the way a Wal-Mart can drive out local businesses. But this assumes that the Web has a finite amount of space and that location counts. No, let AOL-Time-Warner-MCI-UN build the world's largest site complete with everything from news to gambling. So what? If it's good, we'll go. If not, it's no harder to get to www.mom-and-pop.com than to www.mega-site.com. Distance on the Web is measured by links, so the way to make your site "close" to where your customers are is to get lots of places to point to it. How? By being interesting or worthwhile. That's not how real space works where "location location location" outweighs almost everything—precisely because navigating real space is such a pain. While big companies have an advantage when it comes to location because their fatter wallets can buy better positioning, big sites don't have a leg up on being interesting. In fact, often it's quite the contrary.

———————

Web pages create Web space. This is how lived space works in the real world, although it's harder to see because the abstract idea of measured space is ready to leap into our thinking at inappropriate times.

Measured space is the same everywhere; that is its essence. Lived space is different everywhere; that is its nature. What makes lived space different everywhere you look? Things. Lived space is made by the things in it. Downtown is where the business buildings are. Playgrounds and hiking trails are where the parkland is. The "combat zone," as we called it in Boston, is where the triple-X movie houses are. Move the porn shops into the parks and the business buildings into the combat zone and lived space will be thoroughly changed; though abstract, measured space isn't touched in the slightest.

But lived space isn't merely or even primarily the assemblage of stuff. Rather, lived space has tone, character. This is because the things of the world come with emotional qualities embedded. This is true of big things like buildings but it is also true of the smallest, most trivial of items we encounter day to day. Put aside your philosophical and psychological theories—our "default philosophy"—for the moment and think about the last time you were in your kitchen making breakfast or foraging for a snack. You didn't see shapes with colors. You saw stuff you could eat, stuff you could use to make things to eat, or stuff that stood in the way of eating. In fact, the things of the world show themselves as more than just useful or not useful: they have emotional qualities as well. The thick wool socks we see in our drawer are comforting; the Swiss Army knife we carry in our pocket reassures us that we can handle many small problems; the straight-backed chair by our worktable speaks of the rewards of discipline. The rooms of our dwellings have their own, often quite deliberate, moods. Many people have strong reactions to cellars, but we all have similar, less-attenuated reactions to every room in our house: the warmth and utility of the kitchen, the sociability of the living room, the refuge of the bed-room. In *The Poetics of Space,* the French philosopher Gaston Bachelard pries out the subtle effects of things as common as a kitchen drawer or a closet corner.[9] You read the book and rec-ognize feelings you didn't know you were having.

Things make space. Things present themselves in terms of their emotional quality. Put things together and you're begin-ning to build *places* that have their own affective qualities. Lived space consists of places.

———————

The space of the Web is itself full of places—some are like meadows, some are like drainage ditches, but all are full of char-acter and meaning. The Web is a place.

What sort of place is the Web? Let's take a tour of one of bil-lions of routes we might make for ourselves.

A friend sends you an email recommending www.myrtle. co.uk because "it's cool." And Myrtle looks cool. It turns out that Myrtle is some sort of nontraditional marketing company. There's some low-tech information about their business, but the bulk of the long, scrolling black page is devoted to articles they've written and sites they like. You click on the Adbusters link (www.adbusters.com) because the Myrtle page describes it as an anti-advertising site. It turns out that Adbusters is an activist page that views ads as a corporate weapon of global domination. Back to Myrtle. You see a link to www.zeld-man.com, "The Advertising Graveyard." You poke around there for a while, looking at proposed ad campaigns that were axed by their clients, often seemingly out of timidity. Quite amusing. Back on the Myrtle page we find a link to NetBaby (www.netbabyworld.com), which sounds like it might be some type of virtual infant. Nope, it's a site with interactive games. Cool, but you get tired of playing virtual Ping-Pong after losing 15–0 to the computer. Unlike the Adbusters and Zeldman pages, there are no links on NetBaby to other sites, probably because NetBaby is a commercial site and wants to keep you to itself. Back on Myrtle, you find they recommend an article called "Dust My Broom" by an author listed as RageBoy. You go to the site (www.rageboy.com/index2.html) and find a wacky assemblage of overstatement and outrage. As you poke around the site, you realize this RageBoy character (the nom de plume of author Christopher Locke) can actually write. And he gives you lots of links to explore. You make a note to come back to Myrtle at some point, and you recommend it to a few friends via email.

Not all interactions with the Web are this nondirective; sometimes we just want to go to a site and get the information. Not long ago, I gave a talk touting the Web. Afterwards, a woman came up to me and confessed, rather shame-facedly, "I don't browse very much." I told her about my friend Robert who has been on the Internet since it was called ARPANET and you had to be a certifiable geek to use it. Robert doesn't think of the Web as a place for browsing. He uses it everyday, but only for email and research. The Internet is for him very much just a reference library, and although it has extensive holdings, many of them are unreliable, not to say lunatic. Robert rarely surfs or browses, yet he is one of the original Net prophets. And, I told this woman, I don't spend that much time browsing, either. I'm on the Web all day, but I'm not jumping from link to link, exploring the new world. I'm doing my email and visiting sites recommended by others, with occasional surfing because a link attracts my eye. Lots of people who use the Web heavily are very light on random browsing.

"Whew," said the woman. "I thought I was doing it wrong."

———————

Even if my friend Robert and this woman aren't spending a lot of time randomly browsing, they are still using the mechanism that enables the Web to be the Web: hyperlinks. Hyperlinks are the geography of the Web.

Consider the three places—Adbusters, NetBaby, and RageBoy's site—on the Myrtle site that we explored. What do they really have in common? One is a political site, one is a game spot for children, and one is an idiosyncratic collection of essays by a writer with too much personality for his own good. All that holds them together is that someone at Myrtle found them interesting. For that reason alone, the three sites have been placed near one another, creating a small virtual village of sorts. On the Web, nearness is created by interest.

It can be difficult to comprehend this because distance is so much a part of our normal world. So let's try another thought experiment. Imagine you're in a room full of information about Broadway shows. There are theater posters on the walls, essays on the shelves, and song lyrics on a table. There are also several doors. One is labeled "The Life and Music of George Gershwin." Sounds interesting, so you press the door bell. Instantly, you find yourself in a room containing artifacts relating to Gershwin. This room also has magic doors to other rooms, but, oddly, none back to the room you started in. Now, imagine there are a couple of billion rooms and tens of billions of magic doors. We've just described the World Wide Web—the rooms are Web pages and the doors are hyperlinks.

This is a very weird city we've just imagined. The way these doors work changes the way we build the city. No subways. No streets. No scarcity of real estate to provide advantage to some. No limit to how many next door neighbors you can have. In fact, in this city, nearness loses its symmetry: my Broadway show room may be near (linked to) your Gershwin room, but your Gershwin room need not be near my room. You may not even know that I've brought my room near to yours by linking to it; RageBoy may not know that Myrtle has made his page part of its neighborhood.

This new place, the Web, is marked out by the cumulative choices of every homesteader. No placements are accidental. And, unlike in the real world where if I build a house on the last bit of the beach and you want to also, my decisions about where to locate don't affect your choices at all.

Most tellingly, in this Web city there is no outside, no empty space that contains the whole and arranges the parts. The Web is a public place completely devoid of space.

———————

We began by asking why the Web seems so spatial even though it doesn't exist in space. It turns out that our question was confused, as so often is the case with questions that stump us. The Web feels spatial because it's "place-ial," and, because until now all our places have been in space, when we see a place we assume it must exist in space. Then we make a set of assumptions based on taking space as measurable and abstract. What would look anomalous—or just plain weird—in our spatial world makes perfect sense on the Web when we remember the

Web is "place-ial" but not spatial: we can move from place to place but without having to traverse distance; we can arrange places the way we want without worrying about violating the rule that two objects can't occupy the same space at the same time; the symmetry of nearness can be broken.

We are not well prepared for the distinction between space and place. We've come close to it only in literature, movies, and dreams. And except for dreams, generally the space-less places we've visited have assumed that the laws of space are still in effect: Tolstoy can transport us from Paris to Moscow without having us traverse any distance, but the characters in his imagined world are not so fortunate. Nevertheless, in literature, the author can arrange events according to her interests, can build scenes and juxtapose them as she likes, all without having to worry about how they'll physically fit together or how long it will take the reader to travel from here to there. The author, and the reader, enjoy the freedom that comes from the liberation of place from space. The Web is in this sense, like a collective, global work of literature. Or a dream.

———

Traditional space as a container, as the grand "outside" of everything that exists, is essentially passive. But the Web in effect actively holds itself together. If I write a page, it becomes part of the Web, and thus extends the Web place, only if someone links to it. Otherwise, it's simply a page no one will ever find. Through these billions of acts of will the Web is constructed and expanded.

We are not used to this sense of place that creates its own space, although physicists since Einstein are: Newton's idea of space as a giant container has been replaced by the idea—unfathomable to most of us, including me—that the matter of the universe creates the space it's in, and thus the question of what's beyond the universe doesn't make sense. But, of course, the galaxies, unlike the Web, weren't created by human will and don't reflect a patchwork of human interests.

In short, not only is there no outside to the Web, there's also no nature. Everything in it is artificial. So, when we hike through it, we interpret everything we see as purposive. The link to RageBoy's site didn't just grow on the Myrtle page like a tree fungus. We assume there's some sense to the way the pages are arranged and how they're linked. Through Myrtle's links to such an eclectic set of sites, we learn a great deal about Myrtle; and because Myrtle is a marketing company, they certainly knew we would. We also assume purposiveness as we walk down a real street in the real world, but we know that human will was at the service of the necessities of space and so we make allowances. Not on the Web: if the bit is on the screen, it's there because someone wanted it precisely there.

Thus Web "space" necessarily has a moral dimension.

———

And there's an important difference in the politics of space as well. In the real world, I can't just put in a door from my apartment to my neighbor's so that anyone can go through. But that's exactly how the Web was built. Tim Berners-Lee originally created the Web so that scientists could link to the work of other scientists without having to ask their permission. If I put a page into the public Web, you can link to it without having to ask me to do anything special, without asking me if it's all right with me, and without even letting me know that you've done it. RageBoy may wake up tomorrow and find that links to his site have appeared on the pages of people who admire him, who detest him, and who don't understand a word he says. If he doesn't like it, there's nothing he can do about it except ask politely to have the link removed.

There have been attempts to control the placing of links. Most famously, in April 1997 Ticketmaster, with breathtaking short-sightedness, sued Microsoft because Microsoft's Sidewalk city guides were linking from pages about upcoming concerts to the Ticketmaster page where you could buy tickets for that concert. A less arrogant company would have seen this as a marketing coup; after all, Microsoft was drumming up business for Ticketmaster. But Ticketmaster couldn't get past the sites-are-stores model. Although the direct links to the Ticketmaster concert pages were a convenience for the user, Ticketmaster wanted to drag users through their front door and make them march down all the aisles to get to the bananas. This would have been enough to drive many users to Ticketmaster's competitors . . . if Ticketmaster had competitors. Unfortunately, Microsoft settled the suit and Sidewalk agreed to link only to Ticketmaster's home page, a bigger loss for customers than for Microsoft.

The Web couldn't have been built if everyone had to ask permission first. In the real world, we assume privacy and need permission to enter. On the Web, that flips. The politics of the Web, by its very nature, is that of public rights and public ownership.

We usually think of space as a passive container: what you put inside doesn't change space, and space doesn't change what you put inside. Within this container are places that are themselves containers. Within the places are things that are self-contained.

Web space, on the other hand, is built not around things with neat edges but things that point beyond themselves. Links are all that holds the Web together; without links, there is no Web. The top ten sites are always dominated by search sites like Yahoo that get their value—a multibillion dollar value in Yahoo's case—from pointing away from themselves. Web space is linked, dynamic, poorly edged, explosive.

This means that business has to teach itself new lessons. For example, in real-world merchandising, you want people to stay in your store for as long as possible. You use the inconvenience of space to persuade people to buy straight off your shelves rather than schlep around to your competitors to do some comparison shopping. You hope that if they have to walk down the gadgets aisle to get to the bananas, they may decide to buy the device that lets you scramble eggs without breaking the shells. Then, as your store gets bigger, the inconvenience of space practically requires you to put in a high-margin fast food court where people can rest their distance-weary feet.

These real-world tactics lead companies to think about their Web sites in terms of "stickiness," that is, getting their visitors to stick around for as long as possible. Companies want to replicate on the Web the inconvenience of the real world where space is necessarily sticky—it's easier to shop where you are than to travel somewhere else. Sites such as Yahoo faced this issue early on, for customers at Yahoo were there only to get somewhere else, fast. Yet Yahoo was making money by selling users to advertisers: the more pages on Yahoo a visitor viewed, the more Yahoo could charge its advertisers. So Yahoo decided to become a portal, a collection of sites that provide a wide range of services. (Notice that this use of "portal" is the opposite of what the term actually means: a real portal is something you pass through, whereas a Yahoo-style portal is intended to keep you from passing through it.) Yahoo, in effect, has created a mall in which nearness is the result of ease of access: it's easy to find the merchandise you want and the links are right there.

Other companies have adopted a different strategy to replicate online the inconvenience of real-world space. To make their sites sticky, they avoid links to anything except their own sites. That works fine for sites-of-last-resort offering a quick sale of goods at commodity prices. But otherwise, the fear of links makes a site feel like a dead end on the Web. By becoming a hard-edged object that has no pointers beyond itself, the site makes manifest its self-interest and self-absorption. "Here's a place," it says, "at which only we speak. We're so entranced with ourselves that we don't acknowledge the rest of the world or the reality that maybe you don't find us quite as fascinating as we do." Ironically, of course, customers will find the site not sticky but repellant and claustrophobic.

The real stickiness on the Web isn't inconvenience but interest. Because Web sites are amalgams of buildings and documents, we traverse Web space by reading. The techniques of making written materials interesting are well known and highly developed. In short: if you want your site to be sticky, write interesting stuff.

The Web place is defined by interest the way the real world is defined by the accidents of geography. Interest on the Web is, like Web space itself, explosive, out-bound, digressive. The Web space is the opposite of a container. If a store forgets that, we customers will feel like fireflies being chased by a cruel child with a jar in his hands.

———————

So, is the Web spatial? Yes, that is the fact of our experience of the Web. But if we think of Web space in terms of the measured space of the real world, or as a universal grid work of uniform units—an even more abstract notion—we'll go hopelessly wrong. In fact, the Web feels spatial because it is a linked assemblage of *places*—meaningful, significant spots, each one different.

This is the Web's nature, for everything on it was put there by a human being for a reason. In building a site, we are saying that we find this topic interesting and we think others will also. Sites that work make manifest their passion. So inevitably the Web is a plenum of places that have meaning and that matter at least to someone.

But on the Web we experience something we can never experience in the real world: places without space. Instead of needing a containing space to enable movement, the Web has hyperlinks. Links are at the heart of the Web and the Web's spatiality. Because the linked pages come from many people, the Web turns into a place larger than we are. It is a public place, a place we can enter, wander, and get lost in, but cannot own. Since place and space have been inseparable in our experience of the real world until now, when we experience the Web's place-ness, we assume that it must also have the usual attributes of spatiality, including the accidental nature of geography. That makes it easy to forget that what holds the Web together isn't a carpet of rock but the world's collective passion.

chapter three

TIME

HERE'S A WAY TO DRIVE YOUR SPOUSE NUTS. As you're walking someplace that feels a little farther away than it should, turn to her (or him, if that's your preference), and say, "We're not even close to getting there." She replies that it's really not so far. This is your chance. Point at a telephone pole that's fifty feet away. "Close?" you expostulate, "Why, we're not even at that telephone pole." As she absorbs this irrelevancy, immediately say, "We're still not at that telephone pole. In fact, we're not even halfway there. We're still not even halfway there. We're still walking and we're not even halfway to that telephone pole." Then, when you finally pass it—and it will seem like forever if you're executing this maneuver properly—pick another object and begin again: "Ok, so we're past that telephone pole. But we're still not past that mailbox. We're not even half way to that mailbox ..." Your spouse is guaranteed to find this truly annoying. Best of all, your kids will pick up on it in an instant and gleefully add it to their arsenal of ways to irk their parents.

Unfortunately, this exercise isn't just a childish trick. Just as we imagine splitting matter until we arrive at an unsplittable unit, we imagine dividing and subdividing time until we can't divide it any more. We call the resulting atom of time a "moment." But although we have good scientific evidence of the existence of atoms, moments are much more elusive. Everyone as a child has, I assume, lain on the ground, looked up at the clouds, and tried to hold onto a single Now. Every time you look, the Now has gone. It might as well not be there. But it has to be there because, if the past has gone and the future isn't yet, the Now is the only part of time that's real. Yet we can't put our finger on it. The thing that's most real, the Now, escapes us. It's maddening.

Yet time, we're told, is a chorus line of these insubstantial Nows. One thing happens after another. Put a red marker on the current Now and tick the right-hand moments to the left, one at a time. That's how time works. For reasons we can't understand, the line moves in one direction only. If we could drive the wrong way on the one-way street of time, paradoxes would kick in and we might end up as our own grandparents or step on a prehistoric butterfly that somehow causes a grade B actor to become the most beloved president of his century.

The fact that time spins impossible paradoxes every time we look at it, we should take as a hint that something is seriously screwy with our Western thinking on this topic. We break time into moments and then try to stick them back together by stringing them like beads on a necklace. We've even built an economy around uniform moments in which hourly workers sell their time in units of an hour and white-collar workers march to the beat of their Palm computers. Deadlines, schedules, meetings, the workday itself—all move to the ticking of time's moments. The Web, on the other hand, reminds us that the fundamental unit of time isn't a moment, it's a story, and the string that holds time together isn't the mere proximity of moments but our interest in the story.*

————————

The least important change in time wrought by the Web is that "Internet time" is supposedly seven times faster than real-world time. That phrase started out as a witticism because of the pretended precision of the multiplier (purposefully reminiscent of the old saw about the age of dogs), but it gets at something quite true: transactions and communications on the Web, unhindered by matter and its inertia, go faster. If the Internet sometimes feels like a Gold Rush, that's due more to the rush than to the gold.

More important than the difference in pace is the difference in control. If, for example, you go to your local Department of Motor Vehicles to renew your license, you'll wait on line until it's your turn. Cut in line and die. Leave the line because you want to have lunch and you'll have to start all over again when you get back. The line is supreme. All hail the line. If, on the other hand, you are able to renew your license online, you'll click over to the DMV page, click on the link to the "Renew"

————————

*I can't talk about time without acknowledging the influence the work of German philosopher Martin Heidegger (1889–1976) has had on me. From his first major work, he placed time—too often considered to be some sort of illusory artifact of consciousness—at the heart of the question of existence. And at the heart of human existence he put "care" (*Sorge* in German), the fact that things matter to us. I find these two ideas to be profoundly true.

page and read the requirements. If you then decide to go for lunch, or to check the online stock prices, or to watch an episode at www.nakednews.com, you can come back to the DMV page precisely where you left off. You are in control of your time on the Web; time there is not like the tick-tocking crocodile that chases Captain Hook.

Web time is threaded. A "thread" is a Web term for a set of messages on a particular topic. The different forms of Web conversation are in fact distinguished by the different temporal natures of their threads. For example, here's sixty seconds of a chat session:

```
13:04   [roy_e_charles] hey, ilona!
13:04   [JaniSSaire] hahaha roy
13:04   [roy_e_charles] welcome
13:05   [JaniSSaire] hiya ilona sis :o)
13:05   [laindia] !HI!! BleuSapphire
13:05   [manisol] That would make the S and that L about
        40 yrs old. So, there you have it.
13:05   [Bleu|Sapphire] heya deeeeee
13:05   [Val21] wanna chat?
13:05   [Bleu|Sapphire] heya roy
13:05   [Bleu|Sapphire] how are you all doing
13:05   [laindia] lol, funny manisol
13:05   [Guest63077] any body have hotmail
13:05   [Bleu|Sapphire] tx allot hon
13:05   [Angry_Man] Hey what Can't I say in this channel. I
        want to know what words aren't allowed.
13:05   [Guest63077] messenger
13:05   [ChUcKrOcK^01] hello . . .
13:05   [roy_e_charles] hahahha, lol, hahaha, lol, that's all
        she ever says to me! sigh!
13:05   *laindia can tell you Angry_Man
```

13:05   [ChUcKrOcK^01] hello. i'm so lonely here. . . .
13:05   [JoeAnAnAs] anything that is considered with sex-
        ual meaning

Even if you understand the signs and symbols here, this is confusing. The numbers on the left indicate the times the various messages were posted. The names in brackets indicate who's speaking. Because so many people are talking at once—there were thirty people in this chat room, although some were "bots" spamming members with offers to talk about sex for a fee—there may be a gap between a comment and a response into which are inserted comments and responses on a different topic. For example, in this fragment of never-ending discussion, Roy is greeting Ilona, who has just joined the chat, but Ilona is never going to know what message of Roy's made JanisSaire laugh. AngryMan was kicked off once for using bad language and now rejoins asking what the impermissible words are. But before he gets an answer from JoeAnAnAs ("anything that is considered with sexual meaning"), Roy has replied to someone about something funny. Meanwhile, Laindia is telling Manisol that his message struck a funny bone, and Guest63077 is looking for someone who uses Hotmail, possibly to ask a question, but any answer that may come will have been interrupted by several other comments and responses. All this is scrolling by at the speed of typing. Simultaneous timelines have been cut into lengths and woven into a crazy quilt.

Likewise, the "shape" of instant messaging is determined by how it exists in time, and not just because IM requires the two conversants to be online at the same time. Because both people can type simultaneously, IM conversations frequently have a two-steps-forward, one-step-back structure as one person responds to the previous comment while a new comment is being entered. And because the transmission of an IM message is simultaneous with the typing of it, you can't do drafts of an IM message as you can with an email. In addition to these two temporal characteristics—the simultaneity of responses and the immediacy of the writing—you will be immediately struck by one more way that time shapes IM if you watch a teenager like our daughter. While using a computer to do her homework, our daughter usually has five or six IM windows open among which she caroms in the intervals between message and response. Because teenagers typically use multiple IM windows simultaneously, IM requires a type of hasty "time slicing" atypical of, say, composing email.

Words may be the stuff of the Web, but time determines its structures. And it's as if as we're trying to fill every available temporal niche on the Web with new types of talking.

"Everything is in flux," said the ancient Greek philosopher Heraclitus. And he said: "You can't step in the same river twice."[1] While pointing out that everything around us is always changing, he also implicitly acknowledges the continuity that we observe amidst all the change: we may not be able to step into the same river twice, but both times there's a river there. In fact, Heraclitus identified one element—fire—as the underlying principle (*Logos*) of the world.

On the Web, Heraclitus's river becomes a thread. Threads bind the flux of the Web into meaningful currents. But Web threads run in two dimensions. Some, like the ones in chat rooms and email, bind messages together across a stretch of time. Others—hyperlinks—stitch together Web places. But even these seemingly spatial threads shape Web time. For example, imagine two dinnertime conversations. The first is from a real-world breadwinner recounting her day:

> Wow, what a day! I was fifteen minutes late because of traffic, which meant I missed Zulin's weekly update at the staff meeting. So, when it was my turn to report, I explained why I thought we had to change direction on the Manning account, not knowing that Zulin had just spent a full fifteen minutes saying why we can't change direction. And then after wasting most of the morning going over Zulin's plans—basically doing his job for him—I grabbed a fajita-burger at the Splash & Laugh. . . .

It's a nice little story that tell events in sequence, all based around the theme "How My Day Was Tough." Now imagine a conversation from someone who's spent her day on the Web:

> I checked my email and had a message from TimCat that really pissed me off, so I wrote this scathing reply—pretty funny, I thought—but she sent it around to her little circle, so I started hearing from them. Also, Jamie sent me a link to this hysterical site where they've taken all the old ad jingles and have hamsters singing them. It's a lot funnier if you see it. But that site had a link to a place that archives still images from the great old TV shows, like Lucy on the candy assembly line. Then there was another message from the guys at Luckyville trying to get me to tell them what my lucky charm is, which really strikes me as stu-

pid beyond imagining. So I checked out who they are by doing
a search on their names, and, amazingly enough, . . .

So far, this reporter has taken us through close to 2 ½ minutes
of her day. It turns out that because real-world space is so hard
to move around in, it provides continuity to our stories of ourselves: our story tells of our day's journey. Hyperlinks, on the
other hand, enable our attention to fly off and provide no uni-
fying theme beyond what seemed interesting for some reason,
any reason. These threads are loosely raveled, more like eddies
in a river than like rivers running through deep-cut channels.
The Web's hyperlinked threads are tied together by interests
untethered from their usual constraints.

———————

Our default philosophy's view of time is analogous to our view
of space. As with abstract space, we imagine dividing time
into a set of uniform units. As with space, there are obviously
uses for this type of uniform, measured time; in particular, it
lets us coordinate our activities, and it enables science to
understand the coordination of causes and effects (at least it
does at the macro level). And, as with the view of space as the
container in which things exist, this measured time is external
to the events within which we live our lives; our lives are
played out against a clock that's ticking in sync for everyone.
That's why uniform time is useful: we're wrapped up in writing a business proposal or playing Go Fish with our kids when
a dinging intrudes, prodding us to move on to some other
activity. The dinging in one sense comes from an alarm clock,
our Palm organizer, or our spouse, but in another sense, it

issues from the uniform time that remorselessly beats its hammer against our world, driving the occasional nail into us precisely on cue.

But for all the immense utility of having an extrinsic, uniform time available to us, we should be careful not to confuse—as our default philosophy has—the measure with the thing measured. The parallel would be to think that mountains not only have minerals, trees, and snow, they also have inches. But an inch is a measurement of a mountain, not a part of a mountain. Similarly, uniform time measures change but is not itself a property of change. As the tide crests, as the groundhog burrows, and as the businessperson runs to the airplane gate, the drumbeat can be heard, but we're the ones beating the drum. Uniform time is a measurement of a more fundamental type of time that we find in our own lives. Just as we saw that our notion of abstract, uniform space obscures how we actually experience space, so too does our view of time as abstract and uniform mislead us about the nature of lived time. Uniform time talks about independent moments, but we never experience a moment outside the story of our lives.

From the beginning of recorded history, we've understood our situation in the world through narrative. (Of course, without narrative there is no history, so the previous sentence is necessarily true.) A story doesn't thread events together like beads on a string; it instead keeps us in thrall by promising us an ending that was there, hiding, in the beginning all along. Our time is bound together by the stories we hear, tell, and tell to ourselves. A story is an expression of how the world matters to us and thus interest, passion, caring—fire—thread our time. Heraclitus was right.

What can be hidden in the real world—that our interests thread our time—becomes more obvious on the Web. When we are on the Web, there's no possibility of thinking that the threads are joined simply by the proximity of events like two entries on an uncomprehending fourth grader's timeline. No, the threads on the Web are there because we made them, because our interests drove us to jump into this discussion or to stick that hyperlink onto our Web site.

Further, we can read a new reminder of an old truth in the distracting nature of the Web: our interests control us more than we control them. We're more like the fish than the fisherman: we're interested in what hooks us. We're passionate about what sets us on fire. We can certainly educate our passions, but doing so is in effect just electing new leaders to replace the old. We generally don't choose what we're interested in. The Web throws that fact in our faces by presenting an immense world of things that range from brightly colored gewgaws designed to snag our peripheral vision to venal ads that appeal to our lizard brain to profound expressions of faith. These are given to us in an environment without restraint and with no urgency beyond our own curiosity. No permission is required or asked. No polite excuses are needed to abandon a page in mid-sentence. Our interests on the Web are unencumbered and uninhibited. Web threads can be even more insubstantial than they are in the real world. We can paddle down Heraclitian rivers that are smaller, shallower, and less likely of having a worthwhile termination.

Consider the differences between the threading of a real-world lunchtime conversation and a discussion forum on the

Web. In a real-world conversation, topics weave in and out. They arise, they branch, and sometimes they reconnect, always an occasion for small delight. Threading is practically a law when it comes to conversations: if you're all talking about, say, the ending of the movie *Deliverance,* you can't suddenly say, "How about those Red Sox?" without seeming terminally distracted or just plain loony. In a conversation without extrinsic purposes, such as closing a deal or kissing up to the boss, our interests drive us from this point to that with a Logos all their own.

Web conversations are also like this, but they aren't just multithreaded; they're hyperthreaded. Although they usually start with a topic that's more formally defined than real-world conversations, because Web discussions may spread out across weeks or months the threads can become entangled. And because Web time is so fragmented, we can pose new topics that are only tenuously related to the declared theme. For example, www.dv.com provides forums for people deeply involved with editing digital video on computers. While the participants are discussing the details of "SMTPE time code through firewire" and "DV25 compositing and special effects for broadcast," it's perfectly reasonable to interrupt with a question only a rank beginner would ask, such as "How do you plug in the damn camcorder?" Posing this type of question in a real-world discussion among digital video aficionados would be rude, for it would derail the conversation; on the Web, a participant can easily decide to help me out without affecting his participation in the forum or the direction of the discussion itself. The conversational branching points are therefore often more tenuous, less tightly bound to the main theme, just as the links on a Web page may be there simply because the author thinks you might find them amusing; if you don't like www.myrtle.co.uk's link to RageBoy's page, no harm done: Myrtle has a dozen others that may hook you.

Web conversations can be hyperthreaded because the Web, free of the drag of space and free of a permission-based social structure, unsticks our interests. The threads of our attention come unglued and are rejoined with a much thinner paste. We flit from site to site, topic to topic, according to no beat but that of our hearts.

———————

If we lift our heads up from the threads in which we swim on the Web, we can see that the Web itself contributes the persistence that enables threads to exist. Compare the Web to the phone system. We can easily develop a conversational thread in a telephone call, but the thread doesn't exist outside our talking. We can't go back to it. We can't point others to it. When we're done with it, it's gone. But on the Web, our conversational threads lie waiting for us. When they're done, they may well be indexed by a search engine where others will find them, perhaps to our embarrassment. The Web carries its history with it as a permanent resource that can be toured or mined. For example, it's so common for people active on the Web to use a search site to hunt for pages that mention them that the activity has been given its own name: ego-surfing. Frequently, one discovers pages and postings from years ago that today are embarrassing. Too bad. That's the nature of the Web's time.

This means the basic picture of time is different on the Web. Our default philosophy presents a picture of a beaded necklace progressing one bead at a time over the knife-edge of the Now. With each tick, one more moment moves across, changing from future to past. The past and future moments are, according to this default philosophy, equally unreachable: you have to wait for the future moments to come, and once they're gone, you cannot call them back. But time on the Web is more like a hand writing than like a necklace being pulled across a blade. Every message posted today not only will be here tomorrow but becomes part of the Web world's going forward. The Web, unlike a communications medium, accretes value. It is the persistent sum of the stories we are telling one another.

And, oddly, each thread, in adding value to the Web, also increases the looseness of the Web's binding, for there is more and more to distract us—more sites to visit, more arguments to jump into, more dirty pictures to download, more pure wastes of time. It is not an accident that the Web is distracting. It is the Web's hyperlinked nature to pull our attention here and there. But it is not at all clear that our new distractedness represents a weakening of our culture's intellectual powers, a lack of focus, a diversion from the important work that needs to be done, a disruption of our very important schedule. Distraction may instead represent our interest finally finding the type of time that suits it best. Maybe when set free in a field of abundance, our hunger moves us from three meals a day to day-long grazing. Our experience of time on the Web, its ungluing and regluing of threads, may be less an artifact of the Web than the Web's enabling our interest to find its own rhythm. Perhaps the Web isn't shortening our attention span. Perhaps the world is just getting more interesting.

chapter **four**

PERFECTION

IN THE YEAR 2000, if you did business with the leading purveyor of stiff-paper greeting cards, you strolled through rows of neatly organized offerings in a well-lit, relentlessly upbeat store. The cards you thumbed through were tasteful: professionally designed and illustrated, printed without blemish. A friendly person behind a spotless counter took your money and handed you your cards in a pretty white bag. Hallmark Cards had indeed established itself in the real world as the hallmark of proper sentiments properly expressed.

On the Web, however, Hallmark was having its tush kicked by a bunch of hippies. That year, Blue Mountain Arts (www.bluemountain.com) was the #4 site on the Web in terms of visitors; it delivered about 40 million cards during the 2000 St. Valentine's Day season. Meanwhile, www.hallmark.com was #38.[1] The Hallmark site reflected the values of Hallmark's real-world stores: neat, professional, safe. But at Blue Mountain, visitors were a-sea in a wash of garish colors, flashing animations, and cheesy graphics.

There was a clue on the Blue Mountain site about what made it so popular. If you clicked on the link to more information about the company, you saw the two founders, Steven Schutz and Susan Polis, showing themselves as they wanted to be seen: a photo of them driving to Woodstock in 1969 in their "freedom car" covered with peace symbols and slogans, and another of them hand-printing poetry posters in 1971.[2] They're proud hippies. In fact, if you zoomed in on their freedom car, you saw that it looked like their home page: the same colors, same broad-stroke graphics, same ethos.

Just as Hallmark achieved dominance—55 percent of the overall market[3]—in the real world through the predictable immaculateness of their offerings, Blue Mountain achieved dominance in e-cards not despite the imperfection of its site but because of it. On the Web, perfection is scary.

In *The Cluetrain Manifesto,* one of my co-authors, Rick Levine, uses as an example a perfectly ordinary interchange of messages on a discussion board. Someone kicked it off by asking if he was overcharged when he took his Saturn in for its 15,000-mile checkup. After several messages in the predictable "You think that's bad? Here's what happened to me" vein, one came in from an employee at a Saturn dealership who concluded: "I personally agree that what happened to you sucks." The rest of his message made it clear that he wasn't an official Saturn spokesperson—he talks about arguing with Saturn about changing their policies, for example—but even without that we would have known that he was speaking for and as himself because had he been an official spokesperson, he would have said something along the lines of: "We regret whatever inconvenience you may have experienced in your recent Saturn Car Satisfaction Program . . ." This language is weird but completely expected. The corporate rhetoric of failure uses phrases such as "We regret . . . ," "Rest assured . . . ," "We appreciate . . . ," and "Please accept. . . ." When it comes to failure, corporations use these formulaic, ritualistic words precisely so that our eyes have no purchase on what's written. We slide right over them thinking, correctly, "Same old BS. Yada yada yada." Business is too embarrassed by failure to talk about it plainly.

The flip side of this is business's insistence on showing us only idealized images of itself. We have all become used to the semantics of marketing brochures. The pictures in the brochure for a hotel, for example, show immaculate rooms inhabited by models so perfect that they don't leave creases on the bed, much less drape their dirty underwear over the back of the chair. When we enter one of these rooms, even though there may well be a brochure on the desk showing the room in its pristine state, we don't march down to the front desk and demand satisfaction because the real room doesn't match the photo. We understand that the photo is a type of idealization: the room as it would look if no one had ever used it. Given that maybe 250 strangers have stayed in this room ahead of us within the past year alone, we expect there to be some scuffs on the linoleum and a tilt to the lampshade.

Even clip art—a library of photos and drawings available for use in slide presentations—almost always paints a picture of impossibly perfect businesses. The models, so carefully balanced in gender and race, and sometimes in age, are beautiful. No belly hanging over a belt, no dandruff on a shoulder. The models like to cluster gaily around someone at a computer and point to what's on the screen, all the while nodding in satisfaction. Sometimes they like to sit at meetings where one person is using his or her hands to make a point and everyone else is nodding sagely. Also, they like to shake hands, indicating that they have sealed another important and mutually beneficial deal. No anger, no boredom, no coffee rings on desks, no slumping socks, no men staring at women's tits, no managers avoiding taking the last cup of coffee so they won't have to make the new pot. The clip art photos that business feeds itself are as perfect as the marketing images that business feeds its customers.

It's not a lie because there's no intention to deceive. We all automatically adjust our expectations downwards just as we do when we hear an ad claim that a car will give us "the ride of our lives." Even though we all see through the idealized self-portrayals, business almost always insists on maintaining the fiction. Business is anal-perfective.

Business's trafficking in the images of perfection works its way down to the individual in the adherence to the theology of professionalism. There are lots of good things to say about professionals: they meet their obligations and treat their clients in a businesslike fashion that is fair and respectful. But that's only part of what makes a person a professional. A professional gets to wear a white lab coat and carry a clipboard, metaphorically if not literally. The lab coat is the outward sign of membership in the priesthood. The clipboard is the outward sign of the professional's methodology, a set of "best practices" that have emerged over time. In the literal case of a clipboard, the methodology is instantiated in forms that get filled in appropriately. Since every service company claims to have "highly trained professionals"—even the Ku Klux Klan boasts on its home page that it's "America's Oldest, Largest Most Professional White Rights Organization"[4]—having a methodology provides some further value and differentiation; it implies that the company has done this type of thing over and over and has it down to a science. That, in any case, is what business wants to believe about itself. As a result, every failure to reach a publicly stated goal is a public humiliation.

Now consider one of the most common Web activities: using a search engine. Suppose you're trying to find how much steel India exported in 2000. You type in your query, guessing words that might be on the page you're looking for, perhaps "India," "steel," "export," and "2000." The search engine displays a page showing what it has decided are the top ten most likely pages that contain those words. It also tells you that it thinks there are over 36,700 pages that might meet your criteria. None of the top ten is exactly right, so you have the search engine display the next ten. Let's say that #14 on the list has the information you're looking for. Success! And yet from another point of view, this has been an embarrassing failure: if someone asked you a question and you gave thirteen wrong answers before hitting on the right one, you would not be filled with a warm sense of accomplishment. If the telephone company's white pages had this error rate, you would never use them. In fact, it's a certainty that if you looked at all 36,700 pages recommended by the search engine, only a handful of them would be what you were looking for. What sort of failure rate is that? Yet it's completely acceptable on the Web.

There are lots of reasons for this. For one thing, we understand that we are asking a search engine to do the impossible: on the basis of a few words, sort through a couple of billion of pages to find precisely the ones we want and don't take longer than two seconds to do it. (Google.com took 0.25 seconds in the Indian steel example.) For another, the mistakes don't seem overly expensive. If you have a slow connection, your tolerance for unsatisfactory results goes down; conversely, if your connection were so good that pages popped on screen as soon as you clicked on them, you could tolerate looking through many more wrong answers.

But there is another reason we tolerate imperfections on the Web. Because it's our Web, made by and for humans, it shares the characteristic that distinguishes us from the gods: fallibility. Of course, as Tim Berners-Lee, the Web's inventor, is reported to have said, the "Web will always be a little bit broken." We are, too.

One of the passages to adulthood must be the time one of your childhood friends says with a triumphal smugness, "You know there can't be a perfect person because that person would be conceited and so he wouldn't be perfect." A discussion then ensues across the camp bunk beds about whether a person could be perfect without knowing that he's perfect. For all its silliness, there's something important about that moment: at least for a few minutes, our imperfection isn't a complaint, it's a description of what it means to be human.

Unfortunately, it's an insight we can easily lose as we're berated for our failings. Humans are by definition imperfect.

Imperfection is what differentiates us from God. We are made in His image, the Western tradition says, but we are an imperfect copy, limited in our knowledge, our goodness, and our days. Because God is perfect, every difference between us and God is an imperfection; if something is truly perfect, any change to it must degrade it. That's what makes a "perfect storm" perfect: it couldn't be any more of a storm. If God is perfect, then He doesn't lack any wisdom and any change to His wisdom can only be downwards. You can't touch perfection without turning it into imperfection.

Perfection used to carry even more weight than that. Just as we've overused "awesome" so that it now means merely "cool," we've also robbed "perfect" of much of its power. Now perfection is just a measure of how good a thing is, whereas it used to be the very definition of a thing. For example, a perfect circle is all circle with no straight lines or squiggly curves; it is fully and completely a circle. The circles we see every day inevitably aren't perfect, so they also aren't *truly* circles. Perfection in this ancient sense isn't just something you get a blue ribbon for; it is where you find the essence of things. The ramifications of this idea have echoed throughout our history. It means that to understand something, you have to consider it in its perfect form—you can't understand circles only by looking at squiggly examples. But because our world is imperfect, we have to look beyond it—perhaps to a realm of pure reason—to understand things. And even if our world were perfect, our human bodies aren't; our eyesight is limited, we can see things from only one viewpoint at a time, and we're prone to all sorts of perceptual errors. Reason thus triumphs over perception. Thus has this view of perfection contributed to a regret that we have bodies, for bodies lead us astray in virtue as well as in knowledge. And bodies wear out way too quickly. These are not problems that incorporeal God has to face.

That's a lot of weight for perfection to carry: it's at the root of knowledge, religion, human morality, and human mortality. It's no accident than in the ages when imperfection was understood as the defining characteristic of humanity, phenomena such as sin, evil, and death were also more vivid, for those are how human imperfection manifests itself. Our current culture is uncomfortable with those terms because we are uncomfortable about acknowledging our imperfection. Although we may talk about death more than we did before Elisabeth Kübler-Ross[5] raised the issue in the 1970s, it's not clear that we're any more accepting of it than we are of our own sexuality after a full year of intensive media coverage of Bill Clinton's escapades. And we still think that our grade school principals are doing their students a favor by telling them that "If you can dream it, you can be it." No, we don't think we're perfect, but we think it's just a matter of time before progress will protect us from every random misfortune to which our flesh is heir. Where once our imperfection defined who we were as creatures, now it merits a shrug of the shoulders followed by an uplifting thought and a comment to maintain our all-important "self-esteem."

Now we come back to the Web. Links don't work. Email messages are misspelled. Discussion boards devoted to medical matters of life and death contain claims so false that they'd be funny if they weren't so dangerous. The site that downloaded in a second an hour ago now takes five minutes. The link you thought would take you to pictures of endangered species instead sinks you into a porno site that sprouts new windows like poison ivy. Where's perfection when we need it?

The imperfection of the Web isn't a temporary lapse; it's a design decision. It flows directly from the fact that the Web is unmanaged and uncontrolled so that it can grow rapidly and host innovations of every sort. The designers weighed perfection against growth and creativity, and perfection lost. The Web is broken on purpose.

In an imperfect world, software can be an island of perfection. Software does exactly what the programmer tells it to do; following laws of logic embedded in the programming language and carefully explicated in the programming language's manual. The line of a program that says a = a + 1 will always add 1 to whatever value is supplied to the variable "a," and if a programmer follows the rules in writing a subroutine that calculates the cumulative interest on a thirty-year mortgage, that subroutine will always come up with the right answer. Unlike the real world, the world of programs is perfectly knowable, perfectly predictable, and perfectly controllable.

But the design assumption of the Internet was that it's an imperfect world. The Internet isn't just a program. It's a physical system that uses hardware and wires. For the Internet to be robust, its designers had to keep in mind that hardware sometimes fails and cables are sometimes cut by overzealous gardeners with their Rototillers set to eleven. The original designers of the Internet understood this well. In a perfect world, a central dispatcher (a piece of software) would know where every bit needs to go and would route each the most efficient way. But that router's every hiccough would have the effect on the rest of the system of a cardiac arrest. So the Internet was designed to have many decentralized routers, each making decisions about where to send packets next. If one of the routers goes offline—for routine maintenance or because a volcano erupts under Topeka—the packets are simply sent to another router. The Internet routes around disruption.

This feels chaotic and messy. Rather than a centralized brain making decisions based on an overview of the entire system, smaller collections of neurons act by reflex with little concern for anything except moving packets one more leg on their journey. The difference is between on the one hand, having your automobile club lay out a map that shows you a direct route from New York to San Francisco and, on the other hand, navigating by asking gas station attendants along the way who give replies such as, "Gosh, I don't know how to get you to San Francisco, but I think you'll be closer if you drive northwest to the next Sunoco station and ask again." The first way works fine so long as the recommended road hasn't been shut down for repaving and there are never any traffic jams—not to mention that every "driver" in this analogy would first have to drive to the automobile club's headquarters to pick up the map. When it comes to packets in a highly dynamic highway system, the stop-and-ask technique turns out to be not only more robust but also more efficient.

This only surprises us only because we have long assumed that centralized power and efficiency go hand in hand. When you look at the systems and institutions that have advanced our culture—education, government, business, religion—the same basic picture emerges: the bigger a system is, the more control it requires. Or, to be more accurate, the more complex a system is, the more control it requires, which means the amount of required control increases even more steeply. So, while it may take only one adult and a sketch on the back of an envelope to build a tree house, by the time you get to a project such as the Hoover Dam, you have not only hundreds of managers but also managers managing the managers; and then you bring in management consulting firms to help manage the way the managers are managing the managers.

Management is good. It brings efficiency and accountability. But we also know that we like building big management structures for other, less honorable reasons. The larger the fiefdom, the more powerful the monarch. If your project gets big enough, you can actually become a pharaoh and have your brains hooked out through your nose and achieve an imperviousness indistinguishable from death. Management is, in short, about power as much as about efficiency. As Edward Tufte has said, "Power corrupts. PowerPoint corrupts absolutely."[6]

Now consider how we would have gone about building the Web had we deliberately set out to do so. Generating the billions of pages on the Web, all interlinked, would have required a mobilization on the order of a world war. Because complexity requires management, we would have planned it, budgeted it, managed it, . . . and we would have failed miserably. If everything had to be coordinated and controlled, we'd still be processing Requests to Join and Requests to Post. We'd have editors poring through those pages, authenticating them, vetting them for scandalous and pornographic material, classifying them, and obtaining sign-offs and permissions to avoid the inevitable law suits. Yet we—all of us—have built the global Web without a single person with a business card that says "Manager, WWW."

Our biggest joint undertaking as a species is working out splendidly, but only because we forgot to apply the theory that has guided us ever since the pyramids were built. Whether we've thought about it explicitly or not, we all tacitly recognize —it's part of the Web's common sense—that what's on the Web was put there without permission. We know that we can go wherever we want on the Web without permission. We know that we can say what we want in an email or on a discussion board without permission. The sense of freedom on the Web is palpable. The Web is profoundly permission-free and management-free, and we all know it.

The result is a Web that's a mess. About thirty-five years ago, Robert Venturi wrote groundbreaking architectural works— *Complexity and Contradiction in Architecture* and *Learning from Las Vegas*[7]—that found value and even beauty in the city of Las Vegas because the city is a natural (or at least unself-conscious) expression of the summation of forces that built it. But even Las Vegas is well organized compared to the Web, for Las Vegas benefits not only from the silent organizing principle of geography but also from its leitmotif: taking money from visitors. The Web encompasses a far wider set of human interests and motivations. Name a reason a person might want to communicate with another and you'll find someone using the Web that way.

If we say that the Web is self-organizing, it's crucial to recognize that "self-organizing" does not imply that the Web is very organized at all. It is not, for example, as consistent, predictable, or purposeful as a protozoan. To say that the Web is organic is to underappreciate organisms. The Web's organization is only and precisely what individuals on the Web want it to be. Some organizational structures are long-lasting, such as the Web site that a big company has sunk millions of dollars into, but many more structures last as long as two cars playing tag on a highway—a quick exchange of emails, a mailing to five friends, a joke that sweeps around the world in eight hours and is forgotten, a link on a page that no one notices and that breaks two days later.

Yet the Web works. It grows without much maintenance. It invents at insane speeds. We can get done what we want, although usually only after clicking down some dead ends. Beyond any reasonable expectation, it works. But it works only because it has remained true to its founding decision: remove the controls and we'll have to put up with a lot of broken links and awful information, but in return we'll get a vibrant new world, accessible to everyone and constantly in the throes of self-invention. The Web works because it's broken.

Brokenness is not just a characteristic of the Web but is one of its persistent topics. Just about every company of consequence has a site with a "sucks" appended to it: GMsucks.com, DunkinDonutsSucks.com, KelloggsSucks.com, even Salvation ArmySucks.com. In many cases, the company has taken the name itself—or bought it from its original owner—to keep it out of the hands of angry consumers. But even this is telling. And if the name has gone, there are always sites that serve the same function, including www.sucks500.com, where you'll find

"You Suck!" discussion boards for each member of the Fortune
500. For example, "Kupplervati" writes:

> I will for the rest of my life tell absolutly everyone who will listen
> and others besides, NEVER HAVE ANYTHING TO DO WITH BANK
> OF AMERICA!! I had several accounts with them for a year or so,
> aside from all of the bullsh*t charges and fees they sucked out
> of me, there is one outstanding situation:

> I had several fraudulent charges palced on my debit card, I files
> a complaint, they refunded the money. Done, right? WRONG!
> For each of the charges they refunded they had previously
> charged my $22 in overdraft fees, these added up to almost
> $200 dollars. I have been trying for over one entire year to get
> this money returned to me, I have made over 75 phone calls,
> talked to over 55 different people, obtained microfilm tran-
> scripts, faxed, left messages, complaints, called managers and
> managers' managers, no response, I have faxed in documents 9
> times, no result, I have written letters, all the time, its the run-
> around and a load of BULL! If you take someone elses money by
> accident, give it back and its ok. If you don't give it back IT's
> STEALING!!!!!!

A board like this can leave a wildly unfair impression: even if
99.999 percent of your 50 million customers are happy, if just
the 500 who are furious with you were each to leave an angry
message on a discussion board, your company would look as if
it had a major customer revolt on its hands. On the other hand,
each message undoubtedly represents some unknown number
of Kupplervatis who didn't bother to write but who nonetheless
resent being treated as merely another faceless consumer.

But being broken is often a source of delight on the Web; it
sometimes even becomes a positive value. The Web actually rev-

els in mistakes, errors, howlers, slips, and foibles. For example, the best source of information about movies is probably the Internet Movie Database (www.imdb.com). Here you'll find complete cast and crew lists for just about every movie ever made, along with plot summaries, awards, and links to reviews. If you want to know who did the make-up on *Mr. Blandings Builds His Dream House,* IMDB will tell you it was Gordon Bau. But each movie also has a link to a page devoted to perceived goofs. Readers can contribute whatever they want. For example, *Casablanca* turns out to be riddled with "continuity" errors:

> A knight on the chessboard disappears momentarily in the opening chess game.
> Rick's tie is suddenly knotted differently when he sees Ilsa in the bazaar.
> When Rick gets on the train after standing in the rain, his coat is completely dry.

Apparently, some people have watched this movie, not wiping away a tear as Rick and Ilsa part, but sniggering while making notes on a yellow legal pad. The Web is a magnet for this type of nitpicking. Take the newsgroup alt.showbiz.gossip, where in between discussing whether Angelina and Billy Bob will break up and why Sharon can't get her latest movie made, contributors pose questions such as "Who had the most fake accent in a major movie?" and "Who is growing old least gracefully?" Similarly, The Smoking Gun[8] scans in paper documents that show the seamy side of celebrities, such as divorce filings that list the opulence of the rich and witless. The Advertising Graveyard[9] publishes ad campaigns rejected by clients, although it's hard to tell whether the point of the page is that the campaigns or the clients were foolish.

Even when fallibility isn't the explicit topic, it is often the subtext of Web phenomena. In October 1999, people began passing around a link to the purported home page of a Turkish accordion player[10] known now and forever simply as Mahir. "This is my page. . . . . . .WELCOME TO MY HOME PAGE !!!!!!!!! I KISS YOU !!!!!" it says at the top of the page. Then came a series of homey photos of Mahir and his friends, with captions such as "I like music , I have many many musicenstrumans my home I can play" and "Who is want to come TURKEY I can invitate. . . . She can stay my home. . . . . . . I speake turkish , english , rusian, I want to learn otherlanguage !"[11]

This obscure site received over a million visits in two days because visitors were recommending it to their friends. Why? The motives may have been different for each visitor, but judging from the media coverage, this was relatively good-natured; condescending, yes, but not particularly mean or angry. The earnest but broken language, the guileless enthusiasm, the very fact that we, the Web, had plucked Mahir out of obscurity all made the site funny. Indeed, that is seemingly how Mahir has taken it. He has restored his site to its unedited form—whoever began the avalanche of emails apparently made a slightly spiced-up copy of the page—and uses his unexpected fame to plead for world peace; on his new site you can vote on what personal possession of his he should auction off next ("Accordion, Sun glasses, loptop . . . ") and whether the proceeds should be used to buy food or medicine for the poor.[12]

Similarly, in March 2001, the Web was swept with a maniacal interest in the phrase "All your base are belong to us," an insanely bad translation of a line from a Japanese video game. The phrase was posted all over the Web in every conceivable variation. Hundreds of photos were doctored to make it appear that the real world was going "All your base" nuts as well.

Of course, it's not just the Web that relishes imperfection. Outtakes have made their way into the credits of many movies, including manufactured outtakes in the movie *A Bug's Life* in which the animated ants "blow their lines." "Blooper" shows are a low-rent staple of television. And many magazines run amusing slipups as fillers or as features on the back page. But fallibility seems capable of causing tsunamis of interest on the Web unmatched in force by what we've seen in the real world. And some businesses are trumpeting their fallibility in a way not seen in the real world.

For instance, Ben & Jerry's, the ice cream company, has a page on its site called "The Flavor Graveyard" where they list the flavors that failed. It's presented with humor and Grateful Dead references and without embarrassment. Software companies such as Microsoft and Sun post their bugs and workarounds without any sense of shame; it's part of the geek ethos. But the most dramatic example, perhaps, is www.shell.com, the home page for the Royal Dutch/Shell Group of Companies. Other companies facing ecological criticisms take the same route on the Web as off: they control the information flow to present a one-sided picture. Ford Motor, for example, runs a page listing their "environmental initiatives" without ever mentioning that their sports utility vehicles are obscene gas guzzlers—even though in May 2000, William C. Ford, the company's chairman, got headlines by publicly stating this obvious fact.[13] Shell has similar pages, but they also host an

open forum on their site on environmental and political topics.[14]
There you can read messages like this one:

> Just so you know, you are still an Amnesty International urgent
> action (see Just Earth, joint Amnesty/Sierra Club project at
> www.aiusa.org/justearth/corporations/shell.html). Did you not
> supply weapons to Nigerian security forces that brutally crack
> down on the Ogoni people? Did you intervene in the execution
> of Ken Siro-Wiwa? Ken was an environmentalist protesting your
> pollution of the Niger Delta and the Ogoni people's homeland.
> His execution and your silence is unacceptable apathy equat-
> able to manslaughter or even murder.

To this, Noble Pepple of Shell responds:

> Thank you for your email to the Tell-Shell Forum. In it, you make
> a number of points which I would like to respond to below.

> First, let me address your statement that Shell is the subject of
> an "Amnesty International urgent action." This is not the case.
> Amnesty International has informed us that their "urgent
> actions" are issued only by the International Secretariat of
> Amnesty International based in London and that such actions
> are directed at individuals, not companies. No such action
> exists in relation to Shell.

Pepple continues in this courteous but stiff way, maintaining
that Shell did speak out before and after Siro-Wiwa's trial, arguing against his execution. Elsewhere, however, the professional
demeanor gives way to real voice. For example, one post reads,
in its entirety:

Rather than spend vast sums on a fake forum why not have some real fucking action.[15]

According to Mark Wade,[16] one of the founders of Shell's Sustainable Development Group responsible for the forum, any Shell employee who wants to reply can. In this case, Clare Harris of Shell wrote:

> In reply to the last message I have to say that I think it's a great pity that you can't find adjectives other than the ones you used to describe what are obviously very strong feelings.
>
> I work in the large team that are involved with bringing our message about engagement and open communication to a wide audience and whilst I debated whether it would be worth my effort I wanted to reply to you . . . [17]

It's apparent that Harris feels hurt that her group's efforts to be open and honest are perceived as a phony PR Band-Aid. The tang of authenticity in her message comes in large part from its lack of polish, as indeed a whiff of inauthenticity is carried by the canned phrases she uses ("bringing our message about engagement and open communication").

How far does Shell go in allowing open discussion? Consider this message:

> I am Fortune Adogbeji Fashe, currently a permanent resident in the U.S. Last year I got a message from home about the death of my father Chief James Fashe. He was on retirement in Evwreni in Delta State where you have one of your flowstations. He was killed and his house razed I learnt as a result of

Shell's activities in the community. I have read Shell's cheap denial and lame excuses for the atrocities the carryout in Nigeria. But I did not expect it would come to this. I just want to know, what is Shell's side of the story and what is Shell doing about it.[18]

Shell certainly might have discretely removed this particular posting, but it stuck by its policy of openness, providing a venue for messages that are unlikely to make it into Shell's next marketing brochure or quarterly report. As the complaints become more personal and more important, the responses have to go beyond professionalism and show the rough edges of the individuals responding. For example, although no one at Shell has yet posted a response to Fortune Fashe, silence is preferable to a reply done in the "professional" manner, for it would probably have sounded like what the Saturn mechanic in Toronto did *not* say:

We regret whatever inconvenience you may have experienced in the murder of your father.

Professional words would inflame the situation. The imperfect words of a real person are required. Companies talk in bizarre, stilted ways because they believe that such language expresses their perfection: omniscient, unflappable, precise, elevated, and without accent or personality. This rhetoric is as glossy and unbelievable as the photos in the marketing brochure. Such talk kills conversation. That's exactly why companies talk that way.

We don't talk so nice on the Web. Not nearly. Post an innocuous message about how to make mayonnaise and you'll not only get fifteen responses giving you "improvements" but also flaming email claiming that you're brain-dead and personally responsible for the death of the rain forests. Violate a rule of "netiquette"—for example, ask a question about Buffy the Vampire Slayer's clothes on a site devoted to *Buffy* plots and you may be told to post your fucking message to the right fucking group, asshole. If you disagree with George W. Bush's politics, you will probably at least claim that he's retarded and may post a page that compares photos of him to photos of chimpanzees. And if your in-house email uses the formal language suited to written letters, your messages will be passed around the company as an example of dorkiness.

The Web isn't just informal. Its informality is in-your-face. In it we hear ourselves being released from impossible ideals of behavior. We get to kick in the teeth the idealized and constricted set of behaviors known as professionalism. And we get to shed the limits imposed by whatever level of "political correctness" we think has gone too far. Professionalism and knee-jerk political correctness both try to make human existence perfectible by limiting its possibilities: we can be perfect businesspeople by restricting our behaviors to those of professionals and we can be perfect citizens by restricting our utterances to those that are safe. This is a predictable tactic for imperfect creatures who find their imperfection embarrassing: redefine downward what it means to be perfect. We perhaps first resorted to this technique with sexuality when we defined as pornographic the possibilities that we didn't want to consider, masking the fact that at one level we're rutting animals happier wet than dry. And just as the Web throws these possibilities back into our face—you simply cannot be on the Web for more than a few weeks without coming across pornographic images you didn't want to see—so it trumpets that professionalism is a role and politesse is an artifice.

The rules of professionalism and polite, PC discourse are necessarily homogenizing. *Letitia Baldridge's New Complete Guide to Executive Manners,* for example, tells us that

> Your Voice Is Good If:
> You have a low, comfortable pitch—that of a secure person.
> You have a clear tone, which lends authority to what you are saying.
> You sound well-paced. . . .
> You have a warm, intimate, vital quality.
> You speak without a regional accent, or if you have one, it is subtle and harmonious.[19]

Having gotten our voices all to sound the same, Ms. Baldridge then tells us "The Conversational Subjects to Avoid," including "Controversial subjects where the players are emotionally involved and have deep feelings," "Lugubrious subjects: death, destruction, torture, starvation, abuse, etc.," and "Rumor and gossip"—in other words, the very meat and potatoes of conversation on the Web.[20] This book, written in 1985 and revised in 1993, sounds as if it comes from another era. And, indeed, it does: pre-Web.

Perfection itself is homogenizing: there's only one way to be a perfect circle and there's only one way to be a perfect Baldridgean executive, but there are an infinite number of ways to be lopsided. The Web, on the other hand, suffers from a hypertrophy of difference. Eccentricity is pursued so vigorously that it evolves into obnoxiousness. Rudeness, even wrongness, rejects the pursuit of an inhuman perfection. Nothing proves faster that you're not a Stepford Wife than cutting a smelly ripper of a fart.

This enforced informality is matched by a demand for perfection in other parts of the Web. If I go to www.llbean.com, check the availability of a teal Fine-Gauge Cotton Crewneck Sweater, and see that it's in stock, I expect LL Bean not to reject my order because they're out of them. If I go to www.yamaha.com and read that the YPR50 digital keyboard has 32-note polyphony, and then if it turns out to have only 24, I will be mad enough not just to send it back but to post a "Yamaha SUCKS!!!!" note at one of the consumer review sites. If I buy a GE ASM24DB air conditioner because www.ge.com told me that it's exactly 26" wide, I'm going to become litigiously furious if it doesn't fit in my 26" window. Where the information is precise, factual, and voiceless, we have very high expectations for the information on the Web. According to a study reported in *InformationWeek* in March 2001, "Over half of customers expect E-mail complaints to be resolved within six hours," even though only 38 percent of sites meet that expectation.[21]

This expectation is representative of the implicit bifurcation of the Web. On the one hand, the Web is a tool of automation from which we expect perfect and immediate obedience. On the other, it is a connection that relishes our breaking free of the computer world of perfected calculations and the business world of perfectly mannered professionalism. Imperfection is our shibboleth on the Web, the sign by which we know we're talking with another human being. Crudeness testifies to our escape from the world of permission, so on the Web we jump around like monkeys without diapers.

The Web celebrates our imperfection, ludicrous creatures that we are. Its juice comes from there being as many points of view as people and as many ways of talking as there are Web pages. The Web is where we can air our viewpoints, experiment, play, and fail, and then get right back on our feet and try again. It is not headed towards agreement. Ever. There isn't one way of thinking or talking or behaving on the Web, and if there were, who'd want to go? The Web would be just a large "information resource," a place where we find answers. But the Web is far more interesting. It will never be perfect—complete, final, total, true without exception, good without hesitation. It is, therefore, a genuine reflection of our imperfect human nature, and a welcome relief from the anal-perfectionism imposed on so much of our real-world lives.

chapter **five**

TOGETHERNESS

ON SEPTEMBER 11, 2001, like most other Americans, I spent the morning in front of the television, switching among the three major networks and CNN, fearing what I would hear next. My wife, my daughter, and I sat passively, trying to make sense of the incomprehensible. After a few hours, the newscasters, out of news, were repeating themselves and filling the air with carefully qualified speculation. So I went online.

In addition to email asking if I had survived, messages began arriving from discussion lists. (Discussion lists conduct conversation through email; sending a message to the list causes everyone on the list to receive a copy.) Two lists in particular became unusually active: one for the ex-employees of a small software company I used to work for and the other for Internet technologists. Both lists turned entirely to the only topic that mattered that day. The ex-employee list became a support group where we could at the very least learn that we were not alone in our shock, anger, grief, and confusion. The technology list became a fact-checker for rumors and reports from the network broadcasts. For example, there happen to be a couple of licensed pilots on the list who discussed whether the sureness of the airplanes' approaches proved that the hijackers were professionally trained, and a gun enthusiast said that the hijackers probably didn't use plastic guns because such guns contain enough metal to set off the security detectors. The Web, in short, drew upon the knowledge of citizens from around the nation and around the world to make us smarter . . . and thus to keep our fears as realistic as possible on an unrealistic day.

The Web also provided points of access to local communities across the country. We heard about bridge closings in San Francisco, jet fighters taking off from Hanscom base in Massachusetts, and the police cordoning an area around government buildings in Albuquerque. These events were too small for the national broadcast networks to notice, but because the stories and observations came from people with genuine roots, they gave a picture we couldn't get by watching the endlessly looped scenes our hearts couldn't credit.

Then, because the Web consists of links among people and hyperlinks among pages, the lists started sharing. Information passed from one list to another. People passed along links to Web sites where survivors could list themselves so that friends and relatives could check on them, and to sites providing pages of photos, reactions from around the world, offers of help and consolation.

While the network broadcasts gave us sound and pictures at the speed of light, the Web became a first-person news network: it connected us, gave us voice, provided context, and located expertise that was better able to make sense of the torn frag-ments of news that were being broadcast at us.

During that horrible day, I felt I was participating in two publics. As members of the broadcast public, we sat facing the television screen while news anchors presented images and explanations, performing well under inhuman circumstances. But as members of the broadcast public, we are invisible to one another and to the person talking to us; we are a faceless mass. As members of the Web public, we talked through our key-boards to people with names, points of view, and sometimes deep knowledge of topics that mattered. They weren't broad-casting to an anonymous, faceless mass; they—we—were con-versing. We may not have been in the same room, but we were in some real sense face to face.

This new type of public can't be understood simply by imag-ining a mob, brightly colored faces pasted on them, stretching from sea to sea. The Web public consists not of a mass but of individuals joined in an enormous number of groups: discus-sion lists as well as all the other ways the Web enables us to asso-ciate. But, because the Web is fond of taking social structures, pounding them to bits, and letting the pieces rejoin themselves, groups—fundamental social units—are reinventing themselves in ways that challenge every assumption about groups in the real world.

We know everyone in our monthly book club, we know most of the people at the Parent-Teachers Association meeting, we know some people and recognize a few more at the annual town picnic, and each of us is just a face in the crowd at the mass rally. The bigger the crowd, the more faceless we each become, mirroring socially the physical fact that faces become smaller and smaller the farther back in the crowd they are. We have a rich set of terms to describe the relationships among people in groups: I *know* the friend I came to the march with, I *recognize* some people from my home town, I've *heard of* the person exhorting us from the rostrum. This formula of facelessness governs our behavior: everyone gets a turn to speak at the book club meeting, but I don't expect the crowd of marchers to "not interrupt me" when I say something to the person next to me.

We're generally fine with this social diminution. It's been the only way to live with others in a mass society: we all become members of this uniquely human group, the public. The public has no formal structure, no leaders, no rites or rules of membership, no objectives, no charter, no dues, but it is undeniably real. And facelessness is a requirement for admission; we think of ourselves as being part of the public precisely when we're appealing to that which we have in common with others. "As a member of the public I demand . . ." prefaces a claim made on the basis of our simply being social animals rather than because of any special standing. We are proud of being unique individuals, yet we understand that when you put us all together, we become something different.

But we can feel the tension between our individuality and our massness sometimes quite clearly. For example, marketing for a hundred years has lived in the heart of the paradox. Marketers want to affect us quite personally. They try to persuade us to part with our money by appealing to the most personal of motives: our desire to be admired, to stay healthy, to breed with the most comely exemplars of our species. But this personal appeal has been addressed through impersonal broadcast media to whom we are all simply consumers, or "gullets with wallets and eyeballs," in the words of Jerry Michalski.[1] Consumers are differentiated by their "demographic segments" reducing us to a few salient characteristics: 18–24 urban males, 35–45 middle-income stay-at-home moms, and so forth. The characteristics defining a segment could, of course, make much less sense than this: if people with the middle initial "J" who sing in the shower respond positively to sky-written ads urging them to buy beanies, they would become the beanie industry's hottest new demographic segment. Marketing reduces each of us to a very low common denominator.

But we resent being pigeonholed that way. Yes, I am undeniably a 45–55 white suburban male, but it's demeaning to see it put down on paper as if that made me like every other 45–55 white guy trapped in the suburbs. And although it may be statistically true that we 45–55 white suburban males will boost our spending on erasable pens if we see a sexy babe touch one to her lips in an ad, we resent the notion that we're programmable. It's bad enough being reduced to a composite portrait; it's worse to be told that at that level we can be manipulated like ants following a pheromone path.

The way we look to marketers, in other words, is precisely how we don't look to ourselves. It's true that as an aggregate, we're predictable—the bartender at the Anarchists Convention can guess precisely how many bottles of lite beer to stock—but it rankles us as individuals.

The paradox of the public, mass individuals, also has a positive side that we sometimes feel quite clearly. For example, we wait patiently online to vote because we think that our individual vote makes a difference. The longer the line, the more successful the democracy, yet the less my individual vote matters. And I have to reduce the complexities of my political thinking—how to live equitably with my fellow citizens—to a choice of only two parties, with an occasional third party available as a guaranteed loser. The "Democratic" and "Republican" choices are a type of lowest-common-denominator politics, as vapid as the marketers' demographic segments.

And yet when I stand in the voting booth, facing choices I'd rather not have to make and cast a vote in an election that will turn out the same if I exit the booth without voting, the fact that I am merely one person in a land of other people is humbling and affirming. I am merely one, but I *am* one. By virtue of being a member of the public, I get to cast a vote equal to everyone else's. By making my choice, I assert the importance of my individuality within a mass context.

Both the positive and negative side of the paradox of the public are based on the simple formula that says there's an inverse relationship between the size of the group and our individuality as participants in it. Rewrite that formula and the rules of groups come unstuck: do we behave at the book club the way we behave at the mass rally or vice versa? How much individuality are we allowed to bring to the party? What would it mean for us to be a member of a group, even a mass group like the public, without giving up our individuality? What would it mean if we could replace the faceless masses with face-ful masses?

Thanks to the Web, we're in the process of finding out.

———————

Everyone knows that Michael Jackson has sex with kids, that Keanu Reeves is secretly married to David Geffen, and that Jamie Lee Curtis is a hermaphrodite. The evidence? Little to none. So why do these "facts" fall so easily from our lips when we're much more circumspect about the people around us? Easy: the Gloved One, Keanu, and Jamie Lee are famous. The gap between The Famous and us is unbridgeable. They are so far removed from us ordinary folks that when we bump into a Famous Person at an airport, we exclaim, "He sneezed, just like a normal person," surprised that The Famous are yet human.

Fame is the counterpart of our culture's mass public. We are so faceless collectively that we assume the person who has retained her or his face while in front of the crowd must be quite unlike the rest of us poor schlubs. The larger and more faceless we are as a crowd, the more fame counts and the more extraordinary the famous are.

Fame in the real world consists of being known by hundreds of millions of people, many of whom may not care about you or your work. I know World Wrestling League names such as The Rock, Mankind, and Chyna, but I don't care one whit about them or their high jinx. I know about Kathy Lee, Ivana Trump, Sarah Ferguson, and Mr. Whipple while wishing that I didn't. On the Web, it's different; people are famous only to the extent to which people listen to them. On the Web, all fame is local.

For example, if you have a question about setting up your home network—one of those simple tasks that grows devilishly difficult all too often—www.helmig.com can usually help you out. There you'll see one of the Web's most garish and amateurishly designed sites. It violates just about every rule of Web design: too many elements competing for attention, each louder than the next; annoying sound effects; pointless animated graphics. Yet it very likely has what you need: step-by-step troubleshooting instructions specific to the operating system you're using. Helmig, whoever he is, takes you by the hand and shows you exactly how to set up your machine so that it can talk to others on your network. If one troubleshooting path fails, Helmig has a link taking you to the next.

This site looks even better when you compare it to Microsoft's pages. Microsoft has packed a tremendous amount of information onto its site, but to find it, you have to know a lot. And when you do find it, it's expressed in technical language that assumes you're a professional network administrator. The site is well organized but sterile and without a single crack in its façade through which a human face can be glimpsed.

Now compare both of these sites to www.melaniegriffith.com, the home page of Melanie Griffith, the pigeon-voiced movie star. Her site looks like a parody of a movie star's self-image. It presents a "magical world" called Avalon, all heavenly gates, misty waters, and harp music. Melanie has cast herself as the "goddess" of Avalon—you can download screensavers and e-greeting cards at the "Goddess Club" and learn about the charities she supports at the "Goddess Giving" page. Elsewhere on the site you can explore "my body of work," look at high-glam family photos, and immerse yourself in the wonderful world of Melanie. Her site does what it needs to do: it extends the presence of Melanie Griffith, Famous Movie Star. We feel lucky to be allowed a glimpse of her divineness.

Helmig is no Melanie Griffith except in one way: both are famous. Yet the nature of their fame is quite different. Every movie fan knows who Melanie is, but Helmig is famous only among those who know him. Of course, the sense in which we *know* Helmig online is different than the real world sense. I've never met Helmig. We've never exchanged email or chatted online. He has no idea who I am even though I've been to his site many times. What I know of him is what he chooses to show of himself on the Web. I know him not through fifth-hand reports in the tabloids or through the careful crafting of an image by professional handlers. I know him through what he has to say. I know him through the particularities of his page. I know him through his interests. His fame consists of some set of people learning what he wants to make public of himself. Fame off the Web usually means that the masses know *of* you; on the Web, fame is earned when people *know* you.

It's not just Web-page providers such as Helmig who become famous on the Web. Local fame is an important driver of the Internet overall. Discussion groups and email lists almost inevitably over time develop a handful of personae who can be counted on to speak frequently and in character. For example, take alt.showbiz.gossip, a Usenet discussion group; at its height, you could rely on Matt Lupo for funny, perfectly aimed comments, Craig Smith for smart-aleck asides about who's gay and who's not, and Miss Lo for feisty replies to critics of her knowledgeable posts. All we know about these people are their typically arch comments. Similarly, on the discussion list for the ex-employees of a software company, even if you have never met David Benjamin in person, you come to expect his infrequent contributions to be consistently hilarious. Because of the exceptional quality of their postings, these people are stars. They are famous. They are celebrities. But only within a circle of a few hundred people. To provide the obligatory twist on Andy

Warhol's ironically enduring comment: on the Web, everyone will be famous to fifteen people.

Fame on the Web is similar to the nature of craftwork; handmade arts and crafts reach orders of magnitude fewer people than the products of mass manufacturers, but they provide a type of local fame because local craftspeople are known in their communities for and by their work. On the Web, the community is defined by interest, not geography, and there is no natural boundary to how large the circle of fame can grow; the local cabinetmaker can make only so many cabinets, but the local Web-page maker can theoretically reach everyone on the Web. And Web fame enjoys an intimacy not typically found in the world of crafts. It's quite common for people famous on the Web to provide access to more personal information. Helmig does; we can find out that he's a forty-one-year-old engineer at Gerber Technology in Brussels and also that he's a *Star Trek* fan who has not "yet" invested in a uniform. Even Melanie Griffith provides a discussion board—for people with substance abuse problems—in which she occasionally participates. Dan Gillmor, a well-known columnist for the print newspaper *San Jose Mercury News,* writes a weblog.[2] Although it's usually more staid than, say, .Zannah's, on December 25, 2000, his entry consisted of a photo of his new niece, Ella. And around the same time, Chris Pirillo, whose daily newsletter, *Lockergnome,* features tips for using Windows,[3] put in a link to an album of photos showing the first Christmas he celebrated with his new wife. Within twenty-four hours, 100,000 people—over half his subscribers—had taken a look at the homey photos. We're not just reading what Gillmor and Pirillo are writing. We're connecting in a way that real-world fame does not permit.

If real-world fame mirrors the facelessness of the real-world public, Web fame is as face-ful as the Web public. If the real-world public reduces us to our lowest common denominator, the Web public consists of an enormous mass of people who are visible only insofar as they are individuals with something to say.

But that doesn't get the equation quite right, for the Web doesn't consist primarily of the famous and their adorers. That's still a one-way fame. More important, the Web is about *groups*—people who, in one way or another, can look into one another's eyes. Groups are the heart of the Web.

Bob Metcalfe presents himself as the ostensive definition of "curmudgeon," belying a decency and personal kindness that surfaces even in one's first interactions with him. Metcalfe, now a gentleman farmer in the surprisingly wired little seaport of Camden, Maine, was the inventor of the Ethernet networking standard and was a founder of 3Com, a leading networking hardware company. But Metcalfe may be best known for the "law" named after him that says the usefulness of a network grows with the square of the number of people that it connects. For example, if there are a hundred people on the telephone network and Fred signs up for a telephone, the usefulness of the telephone system doesn't go up just by one, for now all one hundred current users have one more person they can call. The usefulness, a measure of value, increases exponentially while the number of users increases linearly.

Metcalfe's Law is often cited to remind an audience that increasing the size of a network dramatically increases its value.

It's even given us a way to quantify the importance of the Internet. But in assessing the Internet's value, Metcalfe's Law can obscure the Internet's nature, for the law's mathematics assumes that all points are of equal value and that the connections are made from point to point. This describes the telephone system, but seems to be missing something when it comes to the Web.

Enter David Reed. If you read his personal home page quickly, you'll get the wrong impression of him. It begins: "Dr. David P. Reed enjoys architecting the information space in which people, groups and organizations interact" and it ends with the following description of his "Avocations": "Dr. Reed continues to build and prototype home LANs and portable computer technology in his home laboratory."

Who has heard of a scientist since Dr. Frankenstein who has a "home laboratory"? David is, in fact, a socially conscious, genius-level technologist who has participated in some of the founding events of the personal computer and Internet revolutions. He was there at the beginning when the Net's first wires were connected with duct tape. He was a professor at MIT; later, he was the chief scientist at Software Arts, the company that developed the VisiCalc spreadsheet, the killer app that made PCs worth owning. He went to Lotus as chief scientist where he helped Lotus expand beyond its first spreadsheet, 1–2–3. He's currently an "independent entrepreneur" and consultant. And if you read his home page more carefully, you will see that Reed understands the social relevance of the computing environment he has helped to create. For example, his home page says:

His consulting practice focuses on businesses that want to capture or create value resulting from disruptive dispersion of network and computing technology into the spaces in which people and companies collaborate and partner.

This is Net Geek talk for recognizing that the Internet is the opposite of a hand grenade thrown into a market; it's almost as disruptive, but brings people together rather than tearing them apart. David Reed's interest in groups has guided him throughout his career.

About seven years ago, David was explaining Metcalfe's Law to a skeptical engineer. She understood that the value of the telephone network, measured in potential numbers to call, increases as a square of the number of users. But she pointed out that the number of calls each person makes every day doesn't increase every time a new person joins the network. In fact, the number of calls each of us makes per day probably remains pretty steady as new people join the system. Therefore, she reasoned, the value measured in the total number of calls increases one to one with the increase in the number of users: if the average user makes four calls a day, the total number of new calls per day goes up only by four when Fred joins. That's why the telephone company isn't justified in squaring its bill for services every time they get a new subscriber, even though Metcalfe's Law says that the value of the service has squared.[4]

"Rather than running to the *New York Times* with a breaking news story to the effect that Metcalfe's Law is wrong," Reed says, "I wanted to confirm or refute this law on more fundamental grounds." The "eureka moment" came when he realized that "pair-wise" connectivity—one person to another—isn't the only type of connectivity the Internet affords. There's also the hooking together of individuals into groups. And groups are

one of the major attractions of the Net. People don't join just to
send an email to this or that person; they join to participate in
the hundreds of ways people associate. Reed, being a true geek,
immediately thought about the mathematics of this concept and
realized that the number of potential groups scales even faster
than the number of potential connections: the number of connections is the square of the number of users, but the number
of groups is 2 to the power of the number of users. For example, if 15 people are connected, there are 210 possible connections and 32,768 possible groups.[5] "I realized." Reed says,
"that's why AOL's electronic community was much more sticky
than CompuServe, despite similar content: AOL has more people and thus many more potential groups."

While Metcalfe's Law thinks only about individuals and how
they can connect in undifferentiated ways, Reed's Law locates
the value of the Internet squarely in the presence of groups. The
Net is not a mass market of faceless individuals, or even face-ful
individuals. Rather, it is a complex, overlapping, ever-shifting
set of individuals who have organized themselves into groups of
every sort, including some that are only now being invented.

The range of groups on the Web, as off the Web, is staggering.
You could be a member of a mailing list for people interested in
word origins; someone who regularly plays Quake on a particular server where players start to recognize one another's names;
an active participant in a discussion board that's been up for
over a year and is dedicated to thoughts about one particular
book; a contributor to a travel site where members share experiences; someone who receives progressive filmmaker Michael

Moore's email rants about politics; a friend of Tim Hiltabiddle's to whom he occasionally sends out humor he's found on the Web; a participant in a mailing list for the attendees of a small telecommunications conference; and one of the regular advisors to a guy whose site you like. Each of these groups is different in its constitution, behavior, rules, and longevity. Probably the only thing they have in common is that I am a member of each—and they are all Web-based.

Web groups are different than groups in the real world, and not just because, free of geography, they are often more purely interest-based. Just as important, Web groups are different in time. Consider the difference between the Emily Dickinson Society, which meets once a month in the real world, and Dickinson readers who have found one another on the Web— imaginary examples in both cases. The real-world society sets aside the first Tuesday night of every month to get together. Although individual members may, of course, chat about the Belle of Amherst whenever they run into one another, the group's talk about Dickinson is confined to that two-hour session. Miss it and you've missed it for the month. The Web-based Dickinson group, on the other hand, is held together by a mailing list that lets each member send a message to all the other members. Merry may wake up on Wednesday convinced that a line in one of Dickinson's letters proves that Susan Gilbert was the object of "Wild Nights." She skips breakfast, writes up her idea, and sends it off to the Dickinson list. By the time Merry arrives at work, her message has been received by all 150 participants and two replies already await her. Throughout the day, more messages arrive. The list members read them when they check their email. Perhaps they find the time to dash off a note, or perhaps they come back to it later. The conversational thread is always there, waiting for them.

Threads of discussion take on a life of their own. They may meander and the frequency of contributions may slow, but so long as new messages are coming in, the thread is alive and open. Sometimes threads are explicitly killed: "Take it offline!" someone writes; but more often they simply die of neglect. And on occasion they explode, filling mail boxes with urgent, impassioned messages that beg for replies.

What do we have like this in the real world? A book club meets for a few hours a month. Snail-mail letters going back and forth are slow and connect only two people at a time. A mailed newsletter arrives on the author's schedule and doesn't enable replies from recipients to all the other recipients. Classes on Emily Dickinson occur on a schedule and discuss the topics the professor finds interesting. Chance meetings in the street or the bookstore that lead to conversations about "Wild Nights" are lovely but accidental. Although elements of real-world conversations appear in threaded discussions, there is nothing quite like threaded discussions in the real world.

The differences go down to the details. Imagine the monthly meeting of Merry's book club is held in the dark, a spotlight shining on each person as she speaks. Imagine that the only sound you can hear is that of the person speaking. Imagine that you are unaware of the nodding and the uh huhs and the body language that says your listeners are uncomfortable with what you're saying or that encourages you to say more. This would be a very different sort of meeting. It might encourage you to speak more freely, or it might completely inhibit you; it depends on how you feel about literally being in the spotlight. It might, indeed, encourage you to say more and more outrageous things just to provoke an audible reaction. This would be especially true if you could wear a mask so that the people at the meeting only knew you by a name you chose for yourself—"The Anti-Emily" or "Sweetness and Spice" or "Sappho's Fire" or whatever. Step by step, our old-style meeting has become quite a different sort of beast. And, of course, this is exactly what happens on the Web. For example, if 90 percent of the people on the Dickinson mailing list agree with Merry's thesis about "Wild Nights," Merry may never know it, for it's generally considered bad form to send email that simply says "Uh huh" and "Me, too." These supportive comments, so important in real-world discussions, simply clog the pipes on the Web; no one wants to wake up to thirty-five messages in the "Wild Nights" thread only to discover that thirty-four are from people saying "I agree." So the discussion continues not until most people are nodding and agreeing but until the last remaining antagonist has said the last possible interesting thing. At that point, either the thread dies a natural death or someone says, "You're going down some trivial rabbit hole! Take it offline!"

Most important, because the threads are persistent, they create a new type of public space that enables a new type of participation. Real-world groups often have some process for applying for acceptance, whether it's as casual as asking your book club if your friend Pat can attend or as formal as filling out forms, supplying references, and waiting for the membership committee to vote. They do this because everyone has to fit into a room at the same time; and in the real world you have to filter out the bores because you can't just hit the delete key when they start talking. On the Web, the norm is for groups to be open to anyone who cares to join. What is the membership criterion? Interest. Membership and participation are identical for the most part with Web groups.

That changes the nature of membership. In a normal real-world group, you are either a member or you're not. On the Web, it's common for people to participate by "lurking," reading the postings without posting anything themselves. This is the ultimate in anonymity: not only don't people know who you are but they don't even know you're there. And lurking is considered very good form, for it lets "newbies" absorb the group's ethos and mores.

The laxness of many Web groups about membership can make them as coherent and persistent as the passing lane of a highway. But it also allows these groups to grope towards somewhat persistent forms. For example, for $19.95 a year you can get access not only to each day's *New York Times* crossword puzzle but also to a bulletin board for subscribers. Many of the participants show up only when they're particularly vexed by a clue and may never show up again. Yet, even within this nonce group of random strangers helping one another with the day's crossword, voices emerge as particularly reliable or interesting. And social forms emerge that extend beyond a particular day's chatter; for example, you are asked not to reveal specific answers to that day's puzzle until after noon. If you reply to a request for the answer to a clue, the favored way is to change the font of the answer to white so that it's invisible to people perusing the discussion board for help with other clues. To make the answer visible, you have to use your mouse to "select" the text, causing its color to invert. If you don't know this, you will find the board frustrating, for messages promise answers and then go blank. These rules, forms, and personalities constitute an exoskeleton for the nonce group, another example of the ways small, loosely joined groups on the Web evolve into forms as unpredictable as humans.

————

So the Web version of a traditional real-world group is different in the nature of membership that makes it a group, how it acts as a group, and in the "when" of its existence. In short, the Web has kicked down most of the fencing that lets us recognize a group as a group.

In this new social clearing, types of associations are being created with a rapidity unequalled in our history. From www.k2bh.com that tries to layer virtual relations on top of real-world local communities, to www.jailbabes.com that lists incarcerated women eager for pen pals, the Web is a hotbed of experimental couplings. In fact, the Web sometimes seems to consist of 300 million monkeys chained to Web software development tools and randomly creating new ways for us to be together. The results are, at best, uneven. But we benefit from the Web's ability to evolve new forms so rapidly that if real-world evolution worked as fast, we could move from grapefruit to squid in a couple of months.

Amazon.com's review pages provide a convenient example of the rapid mutation of social forms. The site began with a simple idea: let people post reviews of books. But when bestsellers such as the first Harry Potter book prompted over 3 thousand reviews, the massness of the Web threatened to make the reviews' collected weight more daunting than useful. So Amazon now presents the average rating of the book—from 1 to 5 stars—as a way of harvesting intelligibility from the outpouring of evaluations. But while a 1–5 rating tells us something, it doesn't take advantage of the explicit and often helpful comments that thousands of people were willing to write. To enable readers to find the voices worth listening to in this mass, Amazon added another level of review: readers of the reviews can rate the reviews, indicating whether a particular review is helpful or not. Although there are still 3 thousand Harry Potter reviews to look at, at least you get some guidance about which ones other readers have found worthwhile. Then, with the massness of the Web threatening to outpace the efforts to harness it, Amazon began flagging the reviewers whose reviews were highly rated with a distinctive graphic so that their contributions stand out in the long list. This has the additional effect of making individual reviewers more recognizable. You might remember having liked "Rebecca's" review of *The Scream Museum* when you see her review of *The Viking Claw* because the "Top 50" reviewer graphic makes her comments conspicuous. If you want more context to better understand her reviews, you can click on her name and see a page about her maintained at the Amazon site. It contains a little autobiographical information—she turns out to be a sixteen-year-old who likes science fiction and fantasy, loves *Star Wars* movies, and hopes to write novels for young adults someday—and a collection of all 511 reviews she's written so far.[6] If you find Rebecca's comments helpful, you can add her to your own page on Amazon so that you can keep up with her recommendations. You can also give your own friends access to your page at Amazon, and they can reciprocate; in this way, you can see what your buddies are saying about the books they read. Amazon also surfaces information about the various groupings that naturally occur. For example, Amazon lets you see which groups are buying which books—at this writing, people at Boeing are buying lots of copies of *Body for Life: 12 Weeks to Mental and Physical Strength;* the U.S. Marine Corps is buying *Dungeons & Dragons 3rd Edition Player's Handbook;* the consulting company KPMG is buying *The Beatles Anthology;* Brazil is buying Jerry Seinfeld's *SeinLanguage;* and everyone's buying Harry Potter.

This progression has an almost Hegelian logic to it, each step following from the other, each propelled by an internal contradiction: the Web consists of hundreds of millions of individuals. They are a mass, but each member is unique. Individuals write reviews. The massness of the individuals makes the aggregate of reviews useless. So Amazon captures summary information, 1–5 stars, from the mass of individual reviews. But because those numeric rankings slight the individual side of the Web, the site begins to star the individual reviewers—but by using the masses' review of the reviewers as its criterion. And so on. One can almost feel the breeze from the pendulum as it swings this way or that: massness, individuality, massness, individuality. And, most important, a new relationship between them: the Web consists of a mass that refuses to lose its individual faces.

————————

Never before have we had a public that combines massness with the ability to keep your name and voice and adds the possibility of direct connections among individuals and groups. This has made the Web a playground for new forms of social interaction. Even something as simple as a Q&A format becomes the subject of experimentation. For example, at AskJeeves, a popular

Web-search site, there's a button that links you to AnswerPoint, a site powered by Quiq.[7] Here, visitors can post whatever question they want, and anyone on the planet can choose to answer it.

How do you predict what will happen when you open up a traditional form of interaction to a global forum? The effects are bound to surprise. For example, Kartik Ramakrishnan, one of Quiq's founders, says he didn't expect people to ask the same question four or five times.[8] Then he realized that the users were confusing AnswerPoint with a live chat session rather than understanding that it's a bulletin board where you post a question and wait for an answer. In a live chat, if you ask something and no one replies, you assume you're being ignored; so you ask the question again and again and again. If the AnswerPoint site had made its nature clearer, users wouldn't have made this mistake. But other developments spring straight from the fact that this is a new form of public interaction. For example, Ramakrishnan noticed that "If a question doesn't get answered in three days, the chances of it getting answered decreases exponentially. It gets lost." This is because of the mass-ness of the system: each new question pushes the previous ones down a slot; after three days, a question is usually past the point where all but the hardiest explorers will venture. Likewise, in this mass Q&A system, people's desire to connect one-to-one makes an unexpected appearance. Ramakrishnan found that people frequently use an answer to write a thank-you. "As a result," he says, "two of the five responses to a question may be thank-yous." With so many answers on display, no one wants to bother opening one only to see that it has no new content, just as no one wants to receive 150 emails saying "I agree with Merry" in the Emily Dickinson mail list. A built-in "Thank you" message would drive a lot of "noise" out of the system. Similarly, mailing lists might someday evolve a "Right on!" button that makes it easy for people to nod visibly without choking the mailboxes of those on the list, a function the "Did you find this review helpful?" button serves at Amazon.com. One way or another, through advanced intelligence or trial and error, the system will evolve to meet the seesawing needs of individuality and massness.

The same sort of evolution occurred in the aftermath of the destruction of the World Trade Center, but the day's horror compressed the time scale even further. Only hours after the attack, a site was created at which people in New York City could post their names so that relatives could see they were alive.[9] But the site attracted people who couldn't stop themselves from entering outraged and sometimes racist comments. Within four hours, another Web citizen posted a site that enabled visitors to report people as safe or inquire about someone who was missing without presenting a scrolling list open to abuse.[10] In the most dramatic way possible, the Web evolved ways to enable massive numbers of people to find the faces they cherished and feared for.

———————

As a child, I would gaze out the window of our family's Studebaker trying to grasp that every car we passed had people with their own destinations and their own lives. I find this as incomprehensible as the distances belied by the simplicity of the stars. For example, a few years ago, through one of those everyday familial mix-ups (i.e., I wasn't paying attention), I found myself waiting to pick up my daughter at the Wang Center in Boston when in fact she was at the Schubert Theatre. As I stood in the lobby and scanned the 3,700 faces passing through the doors, I found myself fascinated, almost stupefied, by the fractional insight I was getting into thousands of souls, each different yet the same, each individual yet amassed, each on its way to its own destination, yet each destination within a world we share. I could spend a lifetime with any one of those faces and not know the soul animating it with the depth it deserves.

This is the root of the paradox of the public. It is ultimately a reflection of one of the two abiding human mysteries: there are other people and I am going to die.

We'll leave the second mystery to the Russian novelists. But the first mystery is just as flummoxing (and, of course, closely related to the second): I am the one who hears what I hear, who feels what I feel, who sees things from this precise and exact physical perspective. Not you, not anyone else. I care about myself in a way that I don't care about anyone else. I may not care *more* about myself—I may be willing to sacrifice myself for my family or for the buddy sharing a foxhole with me—but I care about myself in a unique way. I can't ever escape the viewpoint that is mine. Yet I also know that other people value their lives as much as I value mine. I learn, we hope, not only to moderate my own interests but also to find delight in the otherness of others. Everyone from Walt Whitman to Mr. Rogers conspires to teach me this. Ultimately, the world is *shared*. At every instant, our understanding and our behavior are shaped by the fact that there are other people. Even when we're alone, we understand our aloneness in relation to the world of others to which we are going to return. So, if I say that humans are social, I don't mean that we tend to like one another or even that it takes a village to raise a child. I mean simply that we live in a shared world. We are here with others. And that is the condition for there being a public.

Our shared world isn't the surface of the earth. What makes us social isn't shared space, for we share geography with nematodes and macaroons, but we are not *social* with them. What makes us social are shared interests. We care about one another and we care together about the world we've built out of the world we were born into. There should be no need to state such obvious truths. But our history has also brought us to an odd individualism—part of our default philosophy—that says that only individuals are real. Groups, according to this philosophy, are immaterial and thus unreal; a group is really nothing but a collection of individuals. The moral conclusions this default philosophy sometimes draws are as repugnant as its ontological premises are faulty. Without groups, there would be no individual humans, only howling monkeys in human form. In fact, that's unfair to the monkeys. A human being raised in isolation would not be identifiably human in anything except DNA. Sociality grants a mute herd of brutes their souls and selves.

The Web is a new social, public space. But because the Web has no geography, no surface, no container of space that preexists its habitation, we can't make the old mistake about what constitutes our sociality. The Web is a shared place that we choose to build, extend, and inhabit. We form groups there because our interests aren't unique. How could they be if we're truly social? But the ground rules are different from the real world precisely because there's no ground on the Web. In the real world, masses become more faceless the farther away they are. On the Web, each person is present only insofar as she has presented herself in an individual expression of her interests: many small faces, each distinct within the multitude. And since being on the Web is a voluntary activity, we are forced to face the excruciating fact that we spend so much real-world energy denying: *not only do we live in a shared world, but we like it that way*.

You could build a new destiny for your species on an idea as radical as that.

chapter six

KNOWLEDGE

IN CASE YOU WERE WONDERING, Danny Yee thinks *Inventing the Middle Ages* by Norman Cantor is "racy" and "riveting"[1] but Norman Barry's *An Introduction to Modern Political Theory* is inherently flawed because its premise that "Collective words such as 'class,' 'state' or 'society' . . . only have meaning when translated into statements about individual action," is "reductionism carried to absurdity."[2] These are just two of the more than five hundred books Danny has reviewed on his Web site. His index of reviews lists over 120 categories, from "alternative history" to "zoology." In the year 2000, over 500,000 people accessed his home page a total of 1,350,000 times to read his reviews.[3] By comparison—although the numbers are very tricky to compare—the *New York Review of Books* has a circulation of 115,000.[4]

Danny's reviews are straightforward. If he criticizes a book, he explains why and gives examples. He clearly has his preferences, and occasionally even his politics sneak in—his review of John Le Carré's *The Constant Gardener* includes a link to an AIDS action site—but he is consistent and fair. He has a viewpoint, the ability to write, and a readership. What he does not have are qualifications, as he admits on his site's "Frequently Asked Questions" page:

> What are your qualifications?

> None. Well, no formal ones that are relevant to most of my reading—I have an B.Sc. with mathematics and physics majors and honours in computer science. More about me can be found on my home page.[5]

On Danny's home page[6] we learn a little more: He was born in 1969, lives in Australia, and is a part-time computer systems manager for the Department of Anatomy and Histology at the University of Sydney. That's all he chooses to reveal, and finding even that much requires hunting through his site.

Over at CodeGuru.com, Iouri is a different type of authority. In the year since registering at the site, he has posted over 1,100 messages on the discussion boards, answering questions ranging from the introductory to three strides past advanced. The questions come from users of Microsoft's Visual Basic programming language who are stumped enough to admit it in public. They ask questions such as: How do you make an animation, and, more important, how do you make the background transparent? How do you connect a Visual Basic program to a Web browser? How do you maximize the efficiency of a complex application that reads volumes of data to and from a database?

Of the dozens of questions posted there every day, Iouri answers about four on average, making him one of the top three expert posters on the site. And one of the most respected. He seems to know corners of the code no one else has shone a flashlight on. He is Iouri, Code Master.

But, who is Iouri? All we know is what we learn from CodeGuru's "profile" page, where every contributor can exhibit basic biographical information.[7] We learn that his name is Iouri Boutchkine and that he's a systems analyst in New York City. Interesting, perhaps, but you can learn much more about him just by reading a few of his posts. They generally spare no words of introduction, no cheery "I hope this helps!" or "Good luck with your project!" The code he posts is well documented, although you have to be near Iouri's level to understand his explanations; there's no hand-holding of "newbies" here. He signs his messages with his email address, a vouchsafing of trust and a tacit offer of further help. We come to know Iouri through these indirect signs.

Consider a third authority. My wife and I were in the final stages of deciding to buy a new car and had a list of highly specific questions for our local Volvo dealer. Does the "Geartronic" option affect mileage? Is there wind noise from the roof rack? If the trip computer fails, does it affect anything else about the car? Perhaps because we were buying a new model, the dealer was stumped by many of our questions. So we visited www.volvospy.com, where Volvo owners raise questions for group discussion. I posed a question the dealer had answered without much confidence: What is the precise difference between stability traction control and dynamic traction control, other than $1,000? My question stimulated two dozen responses, including a learned discussion of the precise mechanics of each option, as well as some bottom-line advice: in slippery weather, STC cuts down on skidding whereas DTC enables a "performance driver" to take icy corners at 60 mph. I printed out the discussion for my dealer.

Among the people who regularly contribute to VolvoSpy is one who, claiming to be a renegade Volvo dealer, is perfectly frank—it seems—on taboo topics such as pricing. Others exhibit technical prowess in various automotive subsystems. Still others demonstrate a wide array of practical knowledge based on a deep understanding of how Volvos work. For example, you'll find answers from Claudiu Popa to questions about brakes that rub when the car backs up, what the right tire pressure is in various environments, and the effectiveness of fog lights. That is all that we know about him.

There are similarities and differences among Danny, Iouri, and Claudiu. For example, Danny is expressing his opinion, while the effectiveness of Iouri's programming examples can be verified by trying them out; we can learn at least a little more about Iouri from his profile page while we know nothing about Claudiu other than what he writes. But they have one important thing in common: they are authorities without visible qualification. They are Web authorities.

Why on earth would we read them, much less trust them?

———

It's a trust that we know can be easily betrayed. That's why there's a certain sadness in the list of "organizational values" at the Australian government's I-Source National Breast Cancer Centre (NBCC).[8] The very first value is:

Evidence-based. All aspects of the Centre's work are based on the best available evidence.[9]

One can hear the echo of the group's conviction that women are dying because they're treating themselves with remedies backed only by hope, gossip, and auras. After all, the real cases of information overload occur, ironically, when we don't know enough and bad information floods in to fill the void; the size of the void is determined by the depth of human need. The resulting epistemological chaos calls forth sites from authenticating groups such as NBCC.

It is a soberly designed site that reflects the seriousness of its topic. A left-hand navigation bar enables visitors to browse to the expected topics—from risk factors to treatment centers—where they find information and links to more information. But click on the link to the public forum and you read:

> The bulletin board has been removed from the Web Page this month following careful consideration concerning the role of this forum in relation to the overall purpose of the National Breast Cancer Centre. The Centre aims to provide information that is evidence based, and it has become apparent that much of the information posted to the bulletin board was non-evidence based, with many postings actually contradicting evidence based information displayed by the Centre throughout the site. This is confusing to readers, and gives the impression that the Centre is supporting views and information that it does not in fact endorse.[10]

It's easy to see the NBCC's point. Their very own bulletin board was being used to convey the destructive, groundless advice their group was created to counteract. Worse, some read-ers inevitably took the advice as authenticated simply by its show-ing up on the NBCC site. Rather than lead one more reader to harm by printing an herbal nostrum that science knows to be quackery, the NBCC shut down the discussion board.

But, shutting down a discussion board can be like shutting down a city's red-light district: generally you're just pushing the temptation to another part of the city. By keeping its site "pure," NBCC may just be pushing bad information into cor-ners where it won't be contradicted. Not that there's a good answer to this problem. It's possible that we'll someday figure out how to cleanse the Web of pornography and that you will magically never again receive an email that's really an advertise-ment. But the open architecture of the Web guarantees that it will always present bad information. So we will inevitably watch authorities with authoritative knowledge battle to establish their beliefs. While they combat the false statements of charla-tans and liars, they will also be fighting off a more fundamental challenge. It isn't simply that the Web is "democratizing author-ity" so that the power of knowledge shifts to people who, like Danny, Iouri, and Claudiu, become authorities-without-degrees. Rather, what's at issue is why we listen to people in the first place, what we find compelling about what they say.

In short, Danny, Iouri, and Claudiu put meat on the dry bones of knowledge. In so doing, they implicitly repudiate a view of knowledge centuries in the making that in the Age of Computers has reached an unsupportable extreme. In a sur-prising way, when it comes to knowledge, the Age of the Web is correcting the Age of Computers.

If you want to see how we've gone wrong, look at the way we talk about knowledge. Here's one view: "People solve problems by selective, heuristic search through large problem spaces and large data bases, using means-ends analysis as a principal technique for guiding the search."[11] This is from a paper written in 1986 by Herbert Simon, who in 1956 created a theorem-solving program that is generally considered to be the progenitor of artificial intelligence (AI). A theorem-solving program is an example of an "expert system," an AI program constrained to a particular domain of expertise, such as diagnosing diseases or figuring out where to drill for oil. Although there are many approaches to decision-making when designing AI, in most cases the machine examines what it "knows" and assigns numeric weights to various factors and outcomes. If, for example, "measles" scores more points than "poison ivy" because "has a fever" carries a lot of points, then "measles" is the diagnosis.

Simon's description of how we humans make decisions may not seem familiar to us; I couldn't recognize a "problem space" if you gave me a map. Nevertheless, the computer-based understanding of how we make decisions is quite pervasive in our default philosophy, which seems to treat human decisionmaking as a type of expert system. You can see this in the common tag line "Delivering the right information to the right people at the right time." The Google Web search engine reports over 3,550 pages with some variation of that phrase on them. Companies in the hundreds, from Hewlett-Packard[12] to GasTIPS[13] to Autonomy[14] to Bentley Nevada[15]—have employed the phrase to describe the wonders they perform. It is apparently irresistibly attractive. And what could be wrong with delivering the right information to the right people at the right time as an ideal to strive for?

What's wrong is that it misunderstands how humans make decisions. It assumes that good decisions result from good input, just as the familiar computer phrase says: "Garbage in, garbage out." But that's not how humans generally make decisions. It's how we *calculate,* but it's not how we decide. When we make a tough decision, often it's tough because we have too much information and it isn't all consistent. For example, one report says that the market isn't ready for our new product, but another has the market panting for it. One study predicts that the competitive landscape is about to change, but another says it's going to stay pretty much the same. One set of financial projections says costs are going to be outrageous, but another says that they'll be offset by decreases in delivery costs. Making a decision means deciding which of these "inputs" to value and how to fit them together to make a coherent story. In fact, the story helps determine which of the inputs to trust by providing a context in which the inputs make sense. That means the causality runs backwards: the inputs don't determine the decision; the decision determines which of the inputs will count as influences.

Then why do we like the phrase "The right information to the right people at the right time"? Perhaps because it implies that there's a way to eliminate the risk inherent in making decisions and in acting. Of course, that requires conceiving of ourselves as predictable machines made of matter—as computers—rather than as what we feel like to ourselves: an unpredictable disruption of the world of matter.[16]

———

The computer-based view of knowledge that leads us to think of decisionmaking this way is just the latest—and most extreme—version of our culture's knowledge anorexia: it seems that every time we look at knowledge and see something that isn't purely fact-based and objective, we feel bloated and go on a stricter diet.

Knowledge started out fat and chewy. It began with the realization that the world isn't always as it seems. Although the Greeks are usually given credit for this insight, it was also a founding moment for the Hebrews: when Abraham discovered an invisible God beyond the material idols other tribes worshipped, he realized that the truth of the visible world isn't itself visible. Similarly, the Greeks realized that though the world may look one way, its reality is different. For Thales, generally considered the first philosopher, the world *really* was made of water; and Heraclitus said that underneath the apparent constant change is the Logos, a nonapparent principle of change. But the modern concept of knowledge surfaced in Athens, a city of talkers. In the hubbub of voices heard in every market and on every corner, some were saying true things and others were lying, mistaken, or fooling themselves. The Greeks needed to decide who to listen to, who was expressing the hidden truth of the situation, for their government was run by the power of speaking . . . and of listening. "Whom should I believe?" was not merely an academic question.

So they initiated a hunt for the nature of knowledge that has continued for thousands of years. Knowing means more than being right. Plato nailed it when he defined knowledge as "justified true belief." For example, if you guess that Quicksilver will win the Kentucky Derby and he does, you didn't *know* he would win even though you turned out to be right. Knowledge, said Plato, has to be a true belief that we're justified in believing. But what constitutes justification? Thus were 10,000 doctoral dissertations launched.

The argument over justification has continued, thinning knowledge down so that now it's a mere whisper of its former Rubenesque, conversational self. We can (overly neatly) see this in three phases: philosophy, science, and computers.

Philosophers have traditionally upheld the most stringent standards for knowledge because they were trying to found our beliefs on a bedrock of absolute certainty. Descartes's "I think, therefore I am," if not the most famous phrase in the history of philosophy, certainly the most parodied, was just such a bedrock. While this architectural view of knowledge—lay an unassailable foundation and then build a superstructure of knowledge on it—is far less popular today than it was four hundred years ago, the search for certainty is still an important part of the philosophical discipline. Indeed, one effect of its exaggerated concern for certainty has been the general irrelevancy of philosophy, for most of what matters to us and delights us cannot pass philosophy's knowledge-scrutinizing muster.

Scientists, thousands of years after Plato, have a different reason for keeping knowledge lean and fit: they want to learn about the world independent of human and personal biases. In theory, science works simply. Scientists gather facts, often by performing experiments that isolate the causes of events. Scientists then formulate and test hypotheses about how these facts can be explained. Hypotheses are put together into theories that are well proven because their constituent parts—ultimately facts—are well proven. Thus, science describes a world based on evidence and free of personal biases.

During the last half of the twentieth century, this simple picture was dealt two body blows. First, James Watson wrote *The Double Helix*[17] about how he and Francis Crick discovered the structure of DNA. The book portrays scientists as ambitious, competitive schemers rather than noble-hearted, white-coated researchers. Second, Thomas Kuhn wrote *The Structure of Scientific Revolutions*,[18] which brilliantly shows that rather than facts building theories the way bricks build walls, what counts as a fact itself depends upon the theory the scientist is operating under (just as our decisions determine what counts as an "input").

This was the situation as we entered the Information Age. The term *information* was first hijacked by the computer world in the late 1940s when Claude Shannon and Warren Weaver created Information Science. Despite the familiarity of the word "information," this science turns out to be an almost purely mathematical discipline concerned with the most efficient way of moving a pattern of bits from one place to another. It is of tremendous importance to phone companies and other bit-pumping infrastructures, but of no direct relevance to the rest of us who think that information is what you read in a newspaper. Even within the world of normal computer users, "information" isn't just a Shannonesque pattern of bits. As every computer science course teaches, data are the raw, basic facts stored in a computer, and information is an interesting correlation of those facts. Information is fatter than data—the way Cameron Diaz is fatter than Kate Moss. Computer information is still just skin and bones.

There's nothing wrong with bony information. Everyone of a certain age who's worked with a database or an accounting package can remember how much harder it was to maintain employees' records or to process expense reports before there were computers. We used paper forms, staples, folders, drawers, cabinets, and warehouses—entire paper-based cities within our business operations. Computer information was invented because it is so much easier to manipulate than its paper equivalents. But we also know that more and more of business life became a matter of filling in forms and choosing from not-quite-right multiple choices because the computer system required us to do so. The regimentation imposed by computers became standard fare for cartoonists and beatnik poets. We sacrificed the richness and ambiguity of what we know to get something we can manage.

That is, of course, a reasonable tradeoff. But we went much further. We began to take computers as a metaphor for consciousness. You can see this not only in our wholesale adoption of computer terms to describe human capacities—"inputs," for example—but also in our willingness to accept the most absurd stretches of artificial intelligence.

For example, we turned Ray Kurzweil's *The Age of Spiritual Machines*[19] into a best-seller. Kurzweil is a certifiable genius of some sort who put together the teams that invented important and difficult technologies, including the first print-to-speech reading machine for the blind, the first musical synthesizer that could sound like real instruments, and a jazz improvisation program that once kept me entranced for forty-five minutes at Boston's Museum of Science. But the chief value of *The Age of*

Spiritual Machines is, for me, the evidence it gives of how happy we are to go deeply wrong about human consciousness.

A substantial chunk of his book is devoted to showing that "it is reasonable to estimate that a $1,000 personal computer will match the computing speed and capacity of the human brain by around the year 2020."[20] This matters because, Kurzweil writes:

> There won't be mortality by the end of the twenty-first century. . . . Not if you take advantage of the twenty-first century's brain-porting technology. Up until now, our mortality was tied to the longevity of our *hardware*. . . . As we cross the divide to instantiate ourselves into our computational technology, our identity will be based on our evolving mind file. *We will be software, not hardware.*[21]

Kurzweil's premise is that we're essentially software already, but we happen to run on hardware that isn't all that robust. The scary thing is that, regardless of whether Kurzweil is right or wrong, what he says makes sense to us. We may want to quibble about when computers will be that powerful and when we'll be able to record all 100 billion neurons in the human brain, but the premise that we're software slips by us with disarming ease.

The ultimate end of this line of thought is found in an essay by Douglas Hofstadter, best known as the author of the *Gödel, Escher, Bach,* for which he won the Pulitzer Prize.[22] "A Conversation with Einstein's Brain,"[23] published twenty years before Kurzweil's book, presents a thought experiment. Imagine a book each page of which contains all the information relevant to a particular neuron of a particular brain: that neuron's threshold to "fire," which neurons it connects to, and so forth. Imagine that these pages record the precise state of Einstein's 100 billion neurons at the moment before he died. Hofstadter fleshes out this example in some detail and then asks us to imagine that we "say" to the book, "Hullo, Dr. Einstein." We follow the rules in the book for converting sounds into neuron activity; that is, we see which pages to consult and what those pages tell us to do. And we update each page appropriately, for this is a dynamic book. After consulting many, many pages, we come to a set of pages that refer to neurons controlling Einstein's vocal cords, and we consult the rules in the book for converting the firing of those neurons into sounds we can hear. It's "Einstein" saying "Hello" right back at us! Hofstadter's aim is to convince us, in effect, that the book does what Kurzweil's computer will do: it captures the full state of a brain and contains rules for processing new inputs. Thus, argues Hofstadter, the book *is* Einstein in exactly the same way that Kurzweil's computer will be Kurzweil if he lives long enough to dump his brain into his projected $1,000 personal megacomputer; the book combined with our flipping of the pages is a very, very slow computer. Hofstadter seems bent on convincing us that there is no difference between the book and Einstein: both are conscious, both are geniuses, both claim in perfectly good faith to be Einstein.[24]

Our question should be: Why don't we take Hofstadter's book example as an illustration of why computers *can't* be conscious? Could we ask for a more convincing thought experiment to prove that you can't get to consciousness by putting together bits of paper or (by analogy) bits of silicon, no matter how quickly your fingers can flip the bits?

And that's how John R. Searle's famous "Chinese Room" thought-experiment works.[25] It's such a powerful example that it has dogged proponents of artificial intelligence for two decades. In fact, when it was first published in 1980, it was accompanied by twenty-eight replies, most of them objections, from interested parties, many of whom got Searle's point dead wrong.

Searle imagines that he's in a closed room receiving notes from the outside through a slot. The notes are written in what looks to him like gibberish, but he's been provided with a set of rules (in English) that lets him look up the strings of symbols and tells him which set of symbols to pass back out of his little room. He does this long enough to become good at it. It turns out that the symbols coming in are in Chinese and the symbols he's passing out are reasonable replies in Chinese. The people feeding notes into the room are convinced the entity in the room understands Chinese. But Searle entered the room not knowing Chinese and still doesn't have the slightest idea what the notes he's receiving and creating mean.

Why go through this thought experiment? Because Searle, when dealing with the Chinese notes, is doing exactly what a computer does: "As far as the Chinese is concerned, I simply behaved like a computer; I perform computational operations on formally specified elements. For the purposes of the Chinese, I am simply an instantiation of the computer program."[26]

Computers take inputs without understanding them, transform them according to rules based on the form of the input, and produce outputs, just as Searle does. Computers don't *understand* what the bits represent any more than Searle understands the Chinese messages he's reacting to.

Searle goes to all this work to dislodge an idea that should seem implausible in the first place: human consciousness, like a computer, consists of the processing of symbols that are meaningless to it. Rather, Searle concludes, "It is not because I am the instantiation of a computer program that I am able to understand English . . . but as far as we know it is because I am a certain sort of organism with a certain biological (i.e., chemical and physical) structure."[27]

That is, we are conscious because we're animals of a certain sort, and we possess a certain sort of brain and body. Representing the state of a brain doesn't create a thinking mind any more than depicting the actions of a body in a book constitutes creating a life. There's a difference between a biography and a life, and between a representation of neurons and a mind. And there's a difference between the real Einstein who stubs his toe and a book we thumb through that mimics Einstein's neural activity. We could think otherwise only if we have allowed knowledge to become so thin that it doesn't have skin, bones, or any bodily residue at all.

———

A new line of thought in AI explicitly veers from our odd insistence that we are body-less information processors. This alternative view, brilliantly expounded in *Being There* by Andrew Clark,[28] says that the brain is a web of neurons that learns by matching patterns and making associations. For example, we learn to catch a Frisbee without calculating the geometry of its arcing path or forming an inner map of the world with a Frisbee traveling through it. Rather, we associate certain moving shapes in our visual field with successful hand placement, an explanation that accords with the scientific research on the brain. But, asks Clark, how can a network of associations explain how we accomplish abstract and logical thinking? For that, Clark says, the human mind depends upon what he calls "external scaffolding"; that is, we use our bodies to affect the world to help us think. For example, we memorize multiplication tables (a set of associations), but need paper to do complex multiplication problems; we can remember three things to buy at the grocery but use a list to remember twenty; we move the Scrabble tiles around to help us see the possible words; the physicist uses a chalkboard to work out equations that explain the universe's origins. The pen and paper, the Scrabble tiles, and the chalkboard are things in the external world that we alter to help us think. Clark's point is that our advanced thinking, our knowledge itself, is inseparable from the things of the world that we use to help us think and the body that enables us to use those things. Thinking, and thus knowledge, requires not only a brain but also a world and a body. Disembodied software alone is not enough, for our minds aren't apart from the world but fully require engagement with the world, via a body, to do much more than grunt, sneeze, and catch Frisbees.

This is so obvious. The very idea that we could move from flesh to silicon without loss ought to tell us that we have thinned ourselves to an unrecognizable shadow. We've adopted a default philosophy that says we are basically computers that process symbols even though it has required an act of willful ignorance to deny the two facts most evident to us: we *experience* the symbols in a way that bit-flipping machinery cannot and we *care* about what we experience. The computer-based explanation doesn't advance our understanding of what it means to live as a body in a world; it helps us flee from that understanding.

———

Suppose I were to run into one of the disembodied life forms that *Star Trek* crew members encounter repeatedly in their infinity of rerun hell—a wise energy field visible as a static-filled second-rate special effect, accompanied by tinkly, otherworldly background sounds. I sit down and have a nonmaterial beer with it, and it asks me what it's like to have a body. I try to explain what pain and pleasure feel like. "Yeah, yeah," the energy field says, "but what does it *mean* to you to have a body? How does it change who you are?" I pause, clear my beer-addled earthling head, and reply. First, being embodied means caring in a special way about this particular body. After all, in a world full of bodies—from rocks to stars to other people—mine is special. The pain of this body is my pain, the ecstasy of this body is my ecstasy, and, in case we had any doubts about this special relationship, the death of this body is my death. Second, because my body can be in only one place at a time, it has a per-spective. The world literally looks different to you and me because we're looking at it from different angles. But it's also different because being bodily means being born to this family and not that, in this time and not that. The lessons of the body are, then, that it's specially mine, that I care about it, that it is here for a limited amount of time, and that it gives me a unique perspective.[29]

Our idea of knowledge, however, has consistently moved away from the truths of the body. Knowledge, our tradition of thought tells us, is universal, dispassionate, eternal, and objective—exactly what bodies are not. The truths of the body are even taken to be the enemies of knowledge. This basic stance comes with the Greek origins of knowledge: we need the discipline of knowledge because bodily perception can be misleading. Knowing has ever since struck as us a pursuit for ascetics, virgin professors, and nerds uncomfortable in their own skins. Knowing, we've come to believe, is the type of thing that a machine—a computer, or a robot—might do. And it is no accident that the voices of authority that try to shut us up—whether a bad government, a bad teacher, or a bad boss—do so by implicitly claiming to be "realistic," a code word for the claim that the authority sees the world more "objectively" and without the "distortions" of perspective and interest.

It would be ironic, then, if the Web, a world our bodies cannot enter, were to return knowledge to the truths of the body: tied to an individual, oriented by a particular viewpoint, rooted in passion. But, then, irony is the Web's middle name.

———

From the vantage point of knowledge, justification, and authority, the Web is a hodgepodge of ideas that violates every rule of epistemological etiquette. Much of what's posted on the Web is wrong. Much is expressed ambiguously. We are offered justifications that are nonfactual, irrelevant, or patently absurd. Ideas are wrapped in individual voices that make it harder to dig out exactly what's being said. The Web is argumentative. It's belligerent. It's prejudiced. It's funny. It can even be deadly, as in the case of the NBCC. It is the elite's nightmare of hoi polloi, the rabble, the mob, that originally spurred the building of ivy-covered retreats.

But the Web also returns knowledge to its roots in heated arguments in the passageways of Athens. Knowledge isn't a body of truths stamped with a seal of justification. Knowledge on the Web is a social activity. It is what happens when people say things that matter to them, others reply, and a conversation ensues. Unless the conversation is nothing but a set of insults, each person does the human thing of stating why she thinks she's right. That's justification. But the justification may not be canonical. It may take any of the forms that humans use, ranging from the deductive to the intuitive to the breathtakingly stupid. The conversations are self-regulating and self-directing: "If you say one more time that you're right because you just feel that way, then let's just end it here," or "The research you cite comes from a Scientologist with an axe to grind," or "You keep giving scientific-sounding reasons, but you never talk about what's in your heart."

In many of the conversations, we've given up on certainty. Certainty is just too demanding. If that's the only reason to talk about something, then we'll never have an interesting conversation. But certainty isn't a requirement for believing something. Sometimes, we want to believe things that are probably wrong: gossip and idle speculation are all part of the fun. In other conversations, unsubstantiated knowledge can be irksome or harmful, whether it's someone at VolvoSpy.com making up mileage statistics or someone at the NBCC site claiming that garlic cures breast cancer. But we humans aren't that dumb. We understand the body language of opinion more subtly than the practitioners of anorexic knowledge would have us believe: we understand that the statements Danny Yee makes at his book review site are just opinions, that Iouri's programs at CodeGuru may not work or be very efficient, and that someone who responds to our questions at www.VolvoSpy.com may not know much more than we do. We're finely attuned to metadata—information about information. We have to be because so much information is thrown around. We even understand that a table of specifications for a washing machine on the Kenmore site is so reliable that if we buy the washer and it doesn't fit in the hole we have built for it, we can sue Kenmore. We've been sorting through human claims and ideas for millennia. We're actually pretty good at it. But we don't have one standard procedure or a methodology. We just have ways of listening.

This type of conversational listening works best in an environment messy with metadata. We hear the tone of voice, we pick up on the style of the paragraph, we learn from the choice of graphic button, we form judgments based on the links next to the paragraph we're skipping. In reading a Web site, we're also getting a read on the person who created it. We're skilled at deciding which "inputs" are revelatory, just as at the heart of making decisions is the ability to decide which inputs are to be attended to. In short, we don't process information the way philosophers or computer programmers expect us to. We don't use a systematic set of steps for evaluating what should be believed. Instead, we do on the Web what we do in the real world: we listen to the context, allow ourselves to be guided by details that we think embody the whole, and decide how much of what this person says we're going to believe.

So the causality again goes backwards. If we were traditional knowers or information processors, we would gather evidence, listen to arguments and their justifications, and arrive at knowledge, in that order. But the Web is messier and more looping than that. We read backwards and forwards in time, remembering what else we've seen from this person and from others, and anticipating how the story she's telling will unfold. We are not out to grab another handful from a preexisting container of knowledge. Rather, we are using conversation to develop ideas and truths and grand fictions. We are showing one another how the world looks from our perspective—a truth of the body. We are doing so because we care about the world and our place in it—a truth of the body. We are doing so with the urgency of passion—a truth of the body.

We never escaped these obvious truths of the body. How could we? We may ignore them at times because that lets us achieve the goals of science or even because it lets us lord it over others, but science and petty oppression are still realized through embodied people in a world of intelligent bodies. In a truly ironic way, the bodiless Web reminds us of the bodily truths we have always lived.

———

Defining knowledge in the traditional way—true statements that we're justified in believing—is like explaining sex in terms of its ins and outs without ever mentioning that it feels good. When it comes to our cannonballing dive into the Web, we also have to ask: Why do we care enough to want to read this person's page or that person's weblog? And that has at least as much to do with entertainment as with truth.

There are, of course, times when we use the Web strictly as a research library. We want to know whether Martin van Buren was our seventh or eighth president (he was the eighth), how many liters in a quart (1.057), or the driving distance from

Calais to Minsk (1,095 miles). But we can't explain the pull of the Web if we view it simply as an online almanac and gazetteer. What pulls us on is the sound of voices, like the sound of the parties our parents used to throw that we listened to from the top of the stairs. And, just as at a party we migrate towards those who are interesting and we move away from the spouters of facts, on the Web we find those we enjoy hearing from and conversing with.

We thus instantly solve the problem that has plagued computer scientists for decades, a problem the Web has intensified. With all the information available to us, how do we find what's relevant? The problem is that the relevant information doesn't come with a metadata flag flying over it that says "Take me! I'm relevant!" Rather, relevancy is hugely contextual and evanescent. It is extremely difficult for computers to discern what's relevant, as you prove every time you use even the best Web search engines. Because we humans are embodied creatures who care about ourselves and our world, we are able to sniff out relevancy faster than bats find june bugs. But we are attuned not just to relevancy. We are also drawn to what's interesting but perhaps irrelevant, entertaining, or funny. Of course we are, for these are attention-attractors by definition.

In fact, you can look at the Web as consisting of two basic forms of knowledge: the database and the joke. Databases let you look up information. For example, if you want to know what the electrical impedance is of a particular electronic chip, go to www.nsc.com, where the specifications of thousands of chips are stored. Type in the number of the chip and behind the scenes the site creates a database query that fetches the information for you in less than a second. It's actually quite amazing, although not in itself unusual in this modern age. The site can do this because all its information is neatly arranged in a database. Databases aim at predictability and efficiency. They deliver the information that you ask for and expect. If they don't, they're broken.

Unlike databases, jokes, the other form of knowledge on the Web, reveal what you weren't expecting. If they're predictable, they're about as funny as a database. We consult a database because we have an extrinsic interest: we want to know, say, the impedance of a chip because we have an interest in building a radio. Jokes promise their own intrinsic reasons for being interesting, just as does a story or a song. Jokes reveal a link we hadn't seen, an unfolding we hadn't anticipated. Laughter is the sound of sudden knowledge.

The Web is useful because of the database applications that let us look up information, find flights, make reservations, buy books. The Web is exciting not because it gives us the efficiency of databases but because it gives us the punch of a good joke.

Jokes are all about context. They are highly context-dependent—as you will discover if you try telling a joke about family relations in a culture removed from your own—and often succeed because they suddenly reveal something hidden about a context. Jokes are therefore fat. Knowledge, on the other hand, has tried to become context-free and universal. It has tried to become as safe and reliable as a database. While there is obviously a place for safe and reliable context-free knowledge, that's not why we listen to Danny Yee or Iouri or Claudiu. They have no authorization to say what they say, at least none that is presented to us readers. We don't know if they are licensed, have advanced degrees, or have been awarded prestigious medals in their industries. But we listen because, beyond the thin scroll of words on our screen, we hear something rich in them. We're not looking up answers at their sites. We're instead asking questions, listening to responses, perhaps replying ourselves. We are watching knowledge develop. We're drawn for all the reasons humans care about things: we come with an extrinsic concern such as trying to decide whether we should pay a thousand dollars for an option for our car, or we come because the combination of an interesting topic and skilled writing grabs our attention. Frequently our motives are precisely the same as when we read fiction: the story itself pulls us because we are fascinated by the way time can unfold itself, the end finally revealed as present in the beginning. We read with fascination an argument on a topic we don't have a practical interest in because in the words we read both a story and its writers.

The Web is a written world. The 300 million people on the Web are its authors. We get our authority not from degrees and qualifications (all of which could be invented anyway) but from what of us appears in our writing: our authenticity. What is the greatest betrayer of a lack of authenticity? A voice without affect, without passion: a computer program. The knowledge worth listening to—that is worth developing together—comes from bodies, for only bodies (as far as we can tell) are capable of passionate attention, and only embodied creatures, their brains and sinews swaddled in fat and covered with skin, can write the truth in a way worth reading. The bodiless Web is fat with embodied knowledge that could only come from the particular people—smart, wise, opinionated, funny, provocative, outrageous, interestingly wrong—to whom we're listening. Indeed, that's why we're listening.

chapter seven

MATTER

IT'S INTIMIDATING ASKING SCOTT BRADNER a question, especially a simple one. He is one of the "long beards" responsible for the development and maintenance of the core Internet software standards. He was codirector of the project designing the next generation of the basic Internet protocol. He is a senior consultant to Harvard University about its own technological infrastructure and about new technologies on the horizon. As is true of many brilliant engineers, he has little patience for people who spout facts without adequate knowledge. But Scott is fundamentally a teacher; ask him a question without pretence and even his body language commits to explaining the answer until it's understood. So, when I ask him what the Internet is for, it is with some trepidation for it is too simple a question to ask entirely without guile. But Scott takes it at face value and doesn't have to stroke his long beard to think about a reply: "To move bits."

His answer is so simple because it states a mission defined by what it implicitly does not attempt. The Internet is designed to move bits *and not* to decide which bits to move, which bits to block, what is done with the bits, and whether anyone should have to pay for receiving particular bits. It's the Internet's job to allow such capabilities to be added by the people who want them. Thus, by design, all the Internet's bits know is what they need to know to travel from point A to B in numbers that surpass human understanding. In their focus, indistinguishable from stupidity, lies the brilliance of bits: they don't know what information they represent, whether the information is vital to the national security or is just another dumb joke, or who owns the information; all they know is that they need to get somewhere.

But if bits are the stuff of the Net, what exactly are they? A few weeks after our initial conversation, I asked Scott to show me some bits at work. He sent me to meet with John "Jay" Tumas, operations manager at Harvard University's network operations center in Cambridge.

On a chilly spring day, Jay met me outside the building where a few smokers were puffing cigarettes under the protection of an overhang that stopped only the least determined raindrops. We went up a flight of stairs and entered a room that had the sort of wall-sized video display we've learned from the movies to associate with war rooms. But rather than displaying countries and missile silos, this video screen showed a map of the network of machines for which Jay's group is responsible. Even on the oversized display, only carefully calculated plotting kept the machine names from overlapping one another.

Harvard's machines handle lots of bits; in fact, "lots" wildly understates the situation. Until a few years ago, a terabyte was considered the monster number when it came to storing data. If you wanted to get a laugh, you made a joke about needing a terabyte to store something you considered bloated—say, the new version of Windows or the number of spam emails you received a day. But now that the bargain computers you buy at the local appliance store come with disk drives in the double-digits of gigabytes, a terabyte no longer seems to be on the other side of imaginable. After all, a terabyte is "just" 1,024 gigabytes, and with 100-gigabyte hard drives on their way, you and your nine best friends will soon have a terabyte of storage sitting under your collective desks. Nevertheless, a terabyte is a lot of data, equivalent to about a thousand billion typed characters or about 500 million pages of text, enough to fill 40,000 four-drawer filing cabinets,[1] to store about 1 million PowerPoint presentations,[2] to record 250,000 stolen songs, or, if you prefer, to hold 10 million medium-resolution photographs of Pamela Anderson.

Every day, Harvard University transfers from eighty-five to a hundred terabytes of information within its borders and another three to five terabytes to the rest of the world.

Visible through a door in the operations center is the machinery of the Internet, or at least Harvard's contribution to it. Jay began our tour by pointing to a computer mounted on a shelf in a set of adjoined cabinets with black glass doors. "That's the Cisco 12000, the biggest in its class," he said, launching into an explanation that covered OC3, OC48, ATMs, gigabits, and the Hewlett-Packard 6509 before I could stop him. As he unhinged the door to the neighboring cabinet to show me another computer, I stood in front of this silent machine and tried to give myself a sense of its role in the global network.

All over the world in similar air-conditioned rooms, special-ized computers like this one are moving bits. The rooms are well protected, well lit, exceptionally clean, and oddly quiet. The fronts of these computers display small lights, but disap-pointingly, and unlike the lights on computers in 1950s science fiction movies, these don't flicker randomly; the lights in the movies flickered only because we imagined computers working so slowly that the time between bits was perceptible to the human eye.

The Cisco 12000 and computers like it are routers, dedicated to sending packets of information to their next stop on the Internet. They have no monitors, no mice, no keyboards, no hard drives. You can't browse the Web with one of these boxes, and you can't even play solitaire. Yet Cisco recently managed to sell about $8 billion worth in twelve months[3] because routers do one thing magnificently: they stand in front of a stream of bits and like a mad batsman swat them in the right direction—320 billion bits a second in the 12000.[4]

Routers are the beating hearts of the Internet. They are in intimate contact with the Net's lifeblood, packets of bits. Every page you download, every email you send, every MP3 music file you share, every jerky video you view over the Web, every sound or sight that pops up in your browser—each was torn apart at its source, packaged into predictable bundles of bits, and reassembled at the other end.

But there's a problem with bits. They are the stuff of the Web. They are what the Web *really* is, or so it seems. But bits don't exist. At least not in the usual sense. And in the ambigu-ous reality of bits lies the Web's deepest appeal.

———

Descartes has a problem. On the one hand, there's René the Thinker who wants to know any one thing with perfect certainty. On that rock he'll be able to construct an edifice of knowledge; without it, he's left floating pointlessly in a sea of ideas. René the Thinker is a mind in a world of thoughts. Then there's René the Body, a physical object like any other. René the Body leaves footprints, has to open the door before he walks into the next room, and every few hours has to pee. The existence of these two Renés constitutes a problem that has plagued philosophers for millennia: if the stuff of the mind is so different from the physical stuff of the body, how can they interact?

We know that a rolling billiard ball can move another billiard ball by somehow transferring its energy, but we also know that we can't move a billiard ball just by thinking about it. We may not fully understand the physics of energy transfer, but at least we recognize that the two billiard balls are material objects and thus can interact. But thoughts and objects belong to different realms. Thoughts are mental and have no size or weight. How can weightless thoughts ever affect anything in the world? If a feather can't push a billiard ball, how can a mere thought that weighs nothing? How can René's mind raise his physical hand? And it gets worse. If a thought can't push a billiard ball, how can a billiard ball affect our thoughts? How can our minds know anything at all about the physical world?

Don't blame René for this conundrum. Descartes inherited a set of assumptions, as we all do, and was brilliant enough to see how deep a problem those assumptions posed. Philosophy, science, and religion—which, at the time, were not yet fully distinct disciplines—all thought it vitally important to differentiate the mind and body if only because the prevailing European religion said that our souls are not of this earth: things of the earth decay, but our souls last forever. Descartes took the distinction seriously, as had thinkers before him, and came up with an answer: the soul and the body meet—somehow—in the pineal gland. Why this obscure part of our anatomy? The pineal gland sits between symmetrical brain halves, a single structure in an anatomy of pairs, so it was a candidate as the great unifier of spirit and mind,[5] an explanation that shows how desperate Descartes was for an answer.

We may have moved past Descartes's weird glorification of the pineal gland, but we are still confronting the basic problem he identified. Our default philosophy presents us with a sort of solution (although, as we'll see, it comes with some pretty dreadful baggage). The beginnings of our current views are visible in a section of Descartes's *Discourses,* written in the early 1600s. In this work, René pokes holes in everything we believe in order to find the incontrovertible and the undeniable. To convince us that our every perception could turn out to be delusional, he asks us to imagine that an "evil genie" is bent on deceiving us by feeding us perceptions that have nothing to do with reality. Why a genie? It would have been easier for Descartes simply to have us imagine that God is trying to trick us because God has the power to make us sense whatever He wants; but that would have made a liar out of God and a heretic out of Descartes. So Descartes fabricated a being who possesses some of God's power and none of His goodness: an evil genie. Descartes wasn't saying that such a genie exists, only that one might exist; that mere possibility means—Descartes thought—that we can't be 100 percent confident in our perceptions.

If Descartes had been alive at the turn of the twenty-first century, instead of describing an evil genie, he could simply have written: "Didja see *The Matrix*?" When the movie *The Matrix* explains that what we perceive as the real world is in fact a result of the direct stimulation of our neurons by evil aliens, we don't need an explanation of the explanation. It makes perfect sense, although of course we don't think it's actually true. And if Descartes missed *The Matrix,* he could just as well have referred to *The Thirteenth Floor* or any episode of *Star Trek* that features the "Holodeck."

That we accept such a weird possibility so easily is itself remarkable; after all, this idea says that every moment of our experience could be illusory. But the concept fits in well with our default philosophy that says we humans live inside our own mental reconstitution of the world. For example, let's say I see some leaves. The default philosophy explains that light bounced off some leaves and excited nerves in my retina. My brain took that particular stimulation along with inputs about the rustling of the leaves and of their motion, compared it with the other green shapes I've learned to identify as leaves, and said "Leaves ahead!" I thus develop an inner picture of leaves that corresponds to the outer reality. The outer reality exists independent of me—the world would be here even if I were not—while my inner picture applies categories and meanings not actually found in the real world.

This basic idea—our mental life consists of inner pictures of the physical world—shows up in many familiar ideas. For example, we understand insanity as what happens when our inner picture of the world gets severely out of whack with the way the world is. We understand communication as the process of packaging up our thoughts into words and shipping them to another person who unpacks them and thus builds the same picture in his mind. We understand truth as statements that represent, or correspond to, reality. Within the field of artificial intelligence, this idea shows up as the assumption that to make a machine conscious, we have to give its software an inner representation of the external world ... because that's how we think our own "software" works.

Our default philosophy thus attempts to solve Descartes's question about how mental stuff can know physical stuff by saying that our brains transmute the physical world into inner mental pictures. But our default philosophy doesn't accord the physical and the mental the same status. For example, we are likely to say that the mental stuff is merely a representation of what's real, but we can barely find the right grammar to say that what's real is merely the reality of the mental. And we're comfortable saying something like "What we call 'fear' is really just the release of powerful chemicals into the bloodstream," but uncomfortable saying "What we call 'the release of powerful chemicals into the bloodstream' is really just fear." The second sentence hardly makes sense because we are so used to diminishing the mental in favor of the physical. Our default philosophy's picture of how our pineal nature works leads us consistently to devalue the mental.

From here it is but a short and seemingly inevitable step to populating our freshmen dorms with downcast youths who think there's no meaning in life, for meaning itself is something mental that we bring to the real world party. Meaning, our default philosophy says, is something we project onto the real world. The elements of meaningfulness—language, concepts, values—aren't fully real, says our default philosophy, because they don't exist independently of us. So, meaning and reality fall asunder—or, more accurately (according to this view), they can be revealed as never really having been together in the first place. This is what happens to Antoine Roquentin in one of the seminal books of the twentieth century, Jean-Paul Sartre's *Nausea*. Roquentin at a peak moment experiences an old chestnut tree as nothing but a physical mass of twisting roots; the tree's meaning slides off the tree itself. We've probably all been caught off guard by a similarly disturbing moment when a familiar word suddenly becomes just a sound or—on a different scale—a goal we'd been striving for suddenly seems utterly unimportant.

Thus, the picture our default philosophy paints, taken at its most extreme, is bleak. We live alone in our inner representation of reality. We communicate through ambiguous words and hope that the person listening to us is able, at least approximately, to re-create in her own head the ideas rattling around in ours. We supply the world with meaning, blinkered by the accidents of language and history. At any moment, we might wake up and discover that everything we see, smell, or kiss is an illusion caused by a malevolent creature, an evil genie or evil alien, who is directly stimulating our neurons. If all that determines whether our experience is an illusion is whether our experience resembles the real world, then doesn't that say that our experience, our inner picture, is a type of illusion anyway? We're not experiencing the world, we're just experiencing our experience. True illusion or false illusion, it's still just an illusion.

Before we put on our berets and leap into the Seine, however, we should take a moment to remember that our default philosophy does not describe how we live our lives. We may be able to talk ourselves into believing that we're locked in our own heads, projecting meanings onto a meaningless world, but none of that describes an instant of real life. We don't kiss our sensory inputs; we kiss our spouses. We don't live in isolation; we live in the midst of friends and strangers. We don't simply project meanings onto the world; we discover things about the world. Even the quickest glance at how we live shows that our default philosophy is not just inaccurate, it's deeply alienating. And, as we'll see, this alienation is the context that explains why our culture was so ready for the Web that it almost seemed to have been waiting for it.

Move past Descartes by more than 350 years. Nicholas Negroponte is *Wired* magazine's first columnist, a jet-setting member of the digerati, and a dapper professor at MIT's MediaLab. In his book, *Being Digital,* he sees a distinction that seems to mirror the mind-body distinction that vexed Descartes. The world is made of atoms, he says, but digital devices are made of bits. A bit, he says, "is a state of being: on or off, true or false, up or down, in or out, black or white."[6] To illustrate the importance of bits, he tells about the time a receptionist at "one of America's top five integrated circuit manufacturers" needed him to estimate the value of the laptop computer he was about to carry in with him. "Roughly between one and two million dollars," said Negroponte. To the confused receptionist he explained, "While the atoms were not worth that much, the bits were almost priceless."[7]

Given that Negroponte's laptop may well have contained a draft of his best-selling book, we are in no position to argue with his financial assessment. But it is important to keep in mind as we think about the Web that bits aren't the opposite of atoms. In the past few years, we've had a nearly irresistible temptation to think we can take any real-world activity and slap an "e-" in front of it: e-mail, e-commerce, e-business, e-markets. When an "e" doesn't work, we put a "virtual" there instead: virtual sex, virtual workplaces, virtual world. If bits are e-atoms, then this type of mirroring makes sense. But if bits are fundamentally different from atoms, then the world that they compose may be fundamentally different as well . . . and the relationship between the mental and the physical, meaning and things, may not be as broken as our default philosophy portrays it.

Just as you wouldn't understand words if you just looked at them as black marks on a page, you can't understand bits unless you see them in the processes they were designed for. Let's take one bit as it moves through the routers at Harvard. It enters through a copper wire or optical fiber. Somehow the router decides where to send it. How? That requires a story:

Your Aunt Elise got married last week. You made an excuse to avoid flying cross country to attend the wedding of an aunt you haven't seen in fifteen years and never really liked. Now her son, cousin Bernie, has sent you an email saying that he's posted pictures of the wedding on his Web site (and snidely implies that you really should have shown up in person). You go to Bernie's home page and sure enough, there's the phrase "Scenes from a Wedding" and it's in the blue underlined type that indicates a link. You click and see the page with the first picture: Aunt Elise is declining an hors d'oeuvre for the groom, who looks as if he has just realized what he's in for. Although you're not thinking about it at the moment, you understand that the photo you're looking at actually consists of bits sent over the Web from Bernie's site to your browser. The bits in this case encode information about every dot in the photo so that your browser can put them in the right place and show them in the right colors. The bit we're tracking happens to be part of the encoding of the yellowed tip of Aunt Elise's vulpine left incisor.

Here's what's happens. When you click on the link, your browser looks at the source code of Bernie's page; this code says that the link you clicked on points at a Web address, something like "www.BernieandMaude.org/albums/auntelise/photos.html." That phrase is odd, but it's at least vaguely human-readable. Your browser has to translate this into the numeric address assigned to every computer that's home to Web content; this number is like a zip code made so specific that you can ignore the rest of the address above it. But because the list of those numbers is too big and too frequently updated to keep on the computer on your desktop, your browser sends a request to translate "www.BernieandMaude.org" into its numeric address to one of the more than 500,000 "domain name servers" in the world. These computers, which are the equivalent of electronic phone books, list the Internet address of each domain name. The request for the particular page you want makes its way to the computer—the "server"—where that page is stored.

The server reads the file on its hard drive where the photo is kept, and prepares it to move across the Net. An image of 50K, not particularly large in computer terms, contains over 400,000 bits of information. The Web server divides these into packets of about 12,000 bits, preceding each with a "header" containing the information required to get it from here to there, including the destination, the source, and where in the sequence of packets this particular packet belongs. The packets are then sent out over the Internet, directed from router to router until they arrive at your computer; here they are assembled with all the others in the sequence; if a packet is destroyed along the way, this is noted and a replacement is sent.

This oversimplified explanation is essentially correct (hint: if you find yourself quarrelling with pieces of it, you have just tested positive for geekiness), but it also uses a vocabulary of metaphors and convenient fictions such as "address," "request," "destination," "source." If we were to shrink ourselves to the size of a bit and enter a router, we wouldn't see any of these things. We'd just see pulses of energy. At this level, bits aren't sent from the server's hard drive to your computer. Rather, the sequence of bits on the hard drive is reproduced as a series of changes in voltage. This is done in time with the server's internal clock in intervals measured in hundred-millionths of a second. If at a particular tick of the clock a particular line—a wire—inside the computer has an elevated voltage (3 or 5 volts typically), then that bit is taken to be "on," or a 1; if there is no voltage at the tick, then the bit is "off," or is a zero. In between ticks, the state of the wire doesn't matter. In short, at this level of specificity, a bit isn't a unit of "stuff"; it's a characteristic of a wire at a designated moment of time.

These pulses of energy cause the networking hardware in the computer to issue its own stream of synchronized pulses, preceding the sequence read from the hard drive with a sequence of bits that encode the address to which the bits are being sent. But, of course, no *thing* is being sent. Rather, a line is or is not being given a voltage at a particular moment. In a digital environment, this would sound like the fastest one-footed tap dance in history; communications over analog phone lines result in the familiar hiss and pop of modems falling in love.

The packet of bits, a timed sequence of pulses of energy read in tandem with synchronizing pulses on a second wire,[8] arrives at its first router, one pulse at a time, starting with the header information. But a bit that begins a header looks exactly like any other bit. The router recognizes that first pulse as the start of a new packet by recording the value of that bit and then looking at the next seven that come in. If those eight bits form the pattern 0111110,[9] the router recognizes it as flagging the start of a new packet and assumes that the next bits will be a packet's header information, containing the destination address and other data. The router's software has been programmed to look for the dividing points in the header so that it knows, for example, when the destination address ends and the source address begins. In other words, the router performs an act of interpretation. It "takes" one sequence of bits as encoding a destination address. It "consults" a set of "rules" about where to "send" a packet going to that "address." (The rules have to do with an approximation of where the destination is physically located, which wires are less burdened with traffic, and so on.)

Of course, one could take each of these metaphorically expressed activities and resolve it back down to the level of energy pulses. We could replace "address" with "set of pulses" and "consult" with a complex description of the energy states of transistors. We would do so, however, at the cost of understanding what was happening; we'd know the state of millions of transistors, but we wouldn't know that a router is sending a packet of bits to a particular address, much less that a photo of Aunt Elise's wedding is on its way to your browser. To make sense of a bit, we have to look past the physical bit to its role in the language of the network.

But the pineal-like nature of bits—body and soul shaking hands—goes deeper than that. Is a bit merely an energy pulse? No, for I have a piece of wire in my toolbox that has no voltage running through it, and it's not a bit in the "off" state. Nor is a bit a mere "on" or an "off," for I can flip the light switches in my house all day long without their being bits. A bit is only a bit because humans have designed a system to take a bit as standing for something. Those humans created routers to treat pulses as addresses and as data. Bits are only bits because they perform the pineal trick of being physical and mental at the same time. This duality means that human intelligence—and more—pervades the Web down to its smallest building blocks. At no point is the Web merely technology.

———

Bits are far from the only pineal objects in the human neighborhood. Consider *WordWays,*[10] a journal that began publication thirty-four years ago and hasn't changed much since. Four times a year, A. Ross Eckler of Morristown, New Jersey, mails out an issue of about eighty pages. The stiff cardboard cover says it's the *Journal of Recreational Linguistics.* But Eckler has updated the description on the inside of the back cover: *WordWays* is about "recreational logology." Linguistics or logology, the journal is for people besotted with words on the other side of the pineal divide: words as objects. Here you'll find brief contributions of palindromes (seventy-eight from Win Emmons

alone, including "ANA, NAB A SIMIAN—AIM IS A
BANANA" and "YO, BOSS! I, MAGELLAN, A CANAL
LEG A MISS—O BOY!," and anagrams ("Anil" from
Australia contributes "El Dorado" = "lode road," "loathsome"
= "hate looms," and "the ignoramus" = "or math genius.")
Here you'll learn that "automobile insurance" contains all the
vowels exactly twice, as does "educational quotient" and "situ-
ational neurosis." And Fred Crane confesses to his own situa-
tional neuroses: collecting bibliographies of bibliographies of
bibliographies. In a longer article typical of the ilk, Rex Gooch
of Letchworth, England (the names themselves are worth the
price of the issue), poses a challenge to himself: find word lad-
ders (that is, a sequence where one word turns into another by
changing one letter at a time), each "rung" itself being a recog-
nized word, and where the first and last words are seven-letter
heterograms (that is, they contain no repeated letters) and
where the replaced letters occur sequentially, from the first letter through the seventh. And then find ones that work in
reverse sequence. For example: FAINTED-SAINTED-
STINTED-STENTED-STERTED-STERNED-STERNAD-
STERNAL is an example of one with replacements in forward
order. Of course, Microsoft Word flags the last five words as
misspellings, but we can believe Mr. Gooch when he tells us
that they are in the Oxford English Dictionary as "variant
forms."

The *WordWays* authors aren't treating words simply as
objects the way, say, typographers do when they shave curves
and lighten upstrokes as if they were sculpting wood, or when a
stagehand says "Testing one two three" into a microphone, or
when we read the letters on a chart in an ophthalmologist's

office. The contributors to *WordWays* treat words differently, as
pineal, for after decomposing words into meaningless letters,
they recombine them into words legitimized by their inclusion
in one dictionary or another. If real words didn't have to come
out the other side, the puzzles could be solved by any random
grouping; it would be no fun if you could make a palindrome
by mirroring random letters without regard to the words they
form. In this way, *WordWays* treats words much the way routers
treat bits: they are objectified according to rules bounded by
meaning. The complex ways they're treated is determined by
the meanings they carry, whether that meaning is a dictionary
definition for a word or a protocol for expressing Web
addresses for a bit.[11] Words, in short, are as pineal as bits are.
And as pineal as we humans are. And as pineal as the Web is?

The Web obviously consists of billions of dollars worth of computers and wires; its technological basis is one side of its pineal
nature. But in a more important sense, the Web isn't a web of
hardware, or even of bits. It's a web of words. Yes, plenty of pictures adorn the Web, some of them even suitable for viewing by
minors. Increasingly, there are videos and terabytes of music on
the Web. The Internet may even turn out to be the primary way
we transmit television and telephone calls. Nevertheless, the
Web's character comes from text, and that's not likely to change
in the foreseeable future. Words build the place in which the
other forms of media are embedded. Words are the stuff of the
Web.

Words impart their nature to the Web. Although words are
pineal, they aren't mainly physical and "merely" meaningful.

Quite the contrary. They can be words only because they are units of meaning: "hijjengiggle" isn't a word because, even though it can be conveyed through physical marks on paper or through measurable vibrations in the air, it means nothing. Without meaning, a sound isn't a word and marks on paper aren't sentences. The physical side of words is there to serve the meaningful side. (The same is true of bits, by the way.)

Words have always built worlds, just as they build the Web. We sometimes even use them to build worlds—the worlds novels create—that, lacking matter, aren't pineal. That's the paradox built into Sartre's novel *Nausea*. The book tells of a man whose pineal gland seems to be on the fritz, for the real world keeps shaking off its meanings; leaving a mass of undifferentiated perceptions that strikes our hero as slimy and nauseating. Yet, Sartre was a Nobel Prize–winning novelist and *Nausea* is a vividly written work of fiction. Read it and you're in France, seeing the cities of Bouville and Paris through the eyes of the weary historian Roquentin. It's a world of cigarette smoke and crumpled, soggy newspapers lying in the street. Insofar as the book works—and it is a classic of the twentieth century because it works so well—it wraps you in its world.

If you become too depressed, put down *Nausea* and pick up *Huckleberry Finn*. Now you're in the world of a fourteen-year-year-old boy floating down the Mississippi on a raft. The sky, the clouds, the sound of the river, the way a campfire carves out a warm spot in a moonless night, all of this becomes more present to you than the world your body is occupying as you read. The clang of the phone feels like it's calling you back from another world. Words are *Matrix*-like in their ability to create a world. And because the world that words build is constructed entirely out of meanings, not atoms, the meanings can't slide off that world. So long as we're absorbed in reading about Roquentin, Paris isn't going to lose its damp misery, and as long as we're lying next to Huck Finn, the raft isn't going to appear as an alien mass of slimy lumber. The read world is necessarily meaningful because it is made of words. And there's the paradox: Sartre describes a world in which meanings and reality are essentially distinct by creating a world in which meaning and reality are fused. The "matter" of fictional worlds are words in all their meaningfulness.

This is true of the Web as well, although it's obviously not fictional. Because the Web is a written place, nothing is natural there. The words have been chosen on purpose and placed carefully by a human being for some human purpose.[12] Consider two pages that are vastly apart in their content. At www.conspire.com, you'll find fuel for your paranoid conspiracy theories, including a "restored" version of Lee Harvey Oswald's travel itinerary that shows us some trips mainstream historians don't know about. Meanwhile, at Wyatt Wong's Winona Ryder "shrine," the few sentences of text are largely obscured by background photographs of Winona.[13] Yet, considered simply as *written,* these two pages have something important, and quite simple, in common: both sites were created because the authors wanted to share something with others. Despite their difference in content and style, both pages are social acts, written with others in mind. We take that for granted when we visit a site. We understand without having to think about it that the site expresses a point of view. As is almost always the case with so-called "self-expression," these sites express not just someone's inner state but how the world looks to that person. At the simplest level, we understand that these sites were built because their authors care enough about something to take the time to put it down in words; writings are the social expression of passion.

The characteristics of these two pages are precisely, and not at all accidentally, the characteristics of the word-based world of the Web. The Web is a social place. It is built page by page by people alone and in groups so that other people can read those pages. It is an expression of points of view as divergent as human beings. In almost every case, what's written is either explicitly or implicitly a view of how the world looks; the Web is a multimillion-part refraction of the world. Most of all, at the center of the Web is human passion. We build each page because we care about something, whether we are telling other shoppers that our Maytag wasn't as reliable as the ads promised, giving tips on how to build a faster racer for a soapbox derby, arguing that the 1969 moon landing was a hoax, or even ripping off strangers.

In short, what makes the real world real is that it lacks the characteristics that make the Web the Web. The Web is a social place that we humans constructed voluntarily out of a passion to show how the world looks to us. The real world is that which is apart from us; things of the real world are independent of the way we "happen" to take them and the passion that we bring to them. The Web has hit our culture with a force unlike that of any modern technology because of this disjunction. Our passion for the Web is, in a sense, our passion for passion itself.

———

There's no arguing with reality. Things exist independently of our awareness of them, and only a philosopher or lunatic would say otherwise. But our default philosophy's *preference* for what's real over what is "merely" dependent on culture and history itself results from our culture and history. In this sense, reality is a value judgment. But we pay a price for this, since it means rejecting (at least in the abstract) the meaningfulness of the world in which we live: words aren't real, values aren't real, even emotions aren't real because they don't exist independently of their being felt.

When talking about unhappy couples, my mother used to point out that there was a reason they were staying together. No matter how unpleasant the circumstances, each individual is getting something out of it. We can ask the same question about a default philosophy whose values fly in the face of our daily experience: What do we get out of our realism?

First, we get science. Science lets us get closer to seeing the world as it exists without us. Galileo dropped two different weights from the top of the Tower of Pisa and discovered that they hit the ground at the same time. Thus he was able to see that his culture's assumption that lighter things fall more slowly was a filter distorting our view of the real world. The scientific method enables us to drive our assumptions out of the picture by isolating the variables. The scientific method isn't perfect, of course, and the assumptions are often just pushed further down—Stephen Jay Gould's *The Mismeasure of Man*[14] brilliantly shows how racist assumptions skewed the science of anthropology for many decades—but science usually works better than no science at seeing the world as it exists independent of our awareness of it. And with that knowledge comes an unprecedented ability to shape and control our world.

But our realism brings us more than science. We also get to feed our neurotic need to manage the real world. A realist in ordinary terms is someone who doesn't let his (and I use the male pronoun on purpose) personal opinions and wishes get in the way of his judgment. The business manager who takes over a meeting by pulling out a spreadsheet doesn't just objectively lay out a case. No, he uses knowledge, often more a matter of attitude than of content, to shut everyone else up. He now controls the conversation. What's more, he implies that everyone else lacks the guts to face the facts. Optimism in this environment is made to feel like a refuge for dreamers and girly-men. Instead, the realist assumes, we need to "face facts" because then we can manage our fate. In a peculiar way, realism buys us the illusion that we can master a world that is not of our making; we just have to be hardheaded enough. Realism is denial.

The realist often takes tough-mindedness as a virtue. Those he silences are made to feel that they lack the moral fiber to look reality squarely in the eye. Thus, the realist lords it over others not just because of his firmer grasp of the facts but also because of his moral superiority. But although there are certainly times when hardheaded realism is called for, it limits focus to achieve a pragmatic goal. And that's no way to lead your life. Realism is strong medicine that must be used cautiously because it suspends ways of thinking that are essential components of human existence such as dreaming, imagining, supposing, wishing, and hoping. Worse, it presents a view of our relationship to the world that misses the heart of that relationship. Our default realism focuses on the hard-edged things of our world. It is more comfortable with objects having clear and distinct boundaries than with the relationships among things. Ask a realist for an example of a real thing and he will kick the nearest rock because it is bounded, stable, the same no matter what relationship you put it into. Our default realism distrusts relationships because relationships *depend* on the things related: if three stones are aligned, move a stone and the relationship changes; but change the relationship and the stones stay the same. Dependency is taken as a sign of lack of realness. (It is no accident that dependency is taken as weakness in our culture's default psychology as well.) Our default realism carries this thinking over to people; for example, it sees social groups as less real than the people who compose them.

But this once again gets the causality backwards, at least for the relationships that count. Change a stone's relationships and the stone stays the same, but change my relationships, and you change me. Take me out of my relationships, and I don't stay the same. Never put me into relationships—give me no family, no nation, no culture, no language, no religion—and I am not me. To say that we are social creatures is to say that our relationships make us who we are. Knowledge, language, events, even the very perception of real things like rocks, all depend on our living in a world that is a deeply interrelated context of meanings.

Now we go on the Web. By definition, the Web isn't hard-edged. It's hyperlinked. If the basic stuff of the real world is, supposedly, self-contained things like rocks and atoms, remember what the Web has done to its basic stuff, documents. Traditionally, a document is a container. That's why we refer to what a document says as its "contents." Yet this is as unlikely a metaphor as the Web's idea that a document can be a "site." A document, after all, isn't a jar or a pot that has stuff inside; it's

primarily a two-dimensional rectangle with scribbles on its surface. So why do we think a document has contents? Possibly
because we think of ourselves as containers of knowledge and
therefore we see documents as things into which we "pour" our
knowledge so that others can "drink" of it, internalizing it. An
expert is someone who can pour out his or her knowledge, and
a person becomes an expert by taking in the expertise others
have poured out. In fact, our educational system to a large
degree is based on this idea of "transferring knowledge," moving content from the teacher to the student.

But put a document on the Web and it explodes. Rather than
being self-contained, it becomes hyperlinked. A page without
hyperlinks is literally a dead-end on the Web. But this is most
remarkable, for it means that now documents get at least some
of their value not from what they contain but from what they
point to. And some of the most popular and profitable sites,
such as Yahoo.com, acquire most of their value by pointing
beyond themselves. The container—self-contained—model of
the document breaks on the Web. Links rule.

Hyperlinks are not an incidental feature of the Web. They are
what turn the Web from a library of pages into a web.
Hyperlinks make the Web into a traversable place. Rather than
being constructed out of hard-edged atoms and things, the new
world of the Web is built thoroughly and completely out of the
interrelationship of things.

Web relationships go deeper than mere clickable links. As
with the worlds of fiction, nothing on the Web is independent
of us and our meanings and our interests; for this reason, we
can't make the mistake of thinking that what "really" counts is
the stuff that's apart from us. On the Web, there's only passion,

words, and the presence of others, in grand, shifting, ineffably messy relationships. Those connections bind us into something more than we are as individual pieces of organized matter; they are what's most real on the Web. In this, the Web is like the world we live in . . . and is unlike the world as we think about it when seized by a fit of realism. Our default realism is a wildly, even insanely, inaccurate description of human life. The virtual world of the Web exposes more clearly the truth of our everyday lives. That is why the Web—this disruptive technology, this oddball world—feels so familiar and so welcome.

The Web: unreal and proud of it.

chapter **eight**

HOPE

THE WEB IS JUST ANOTHER SET of string and tin cans. In fact, more extreme metaphors are warranted: The Web is a sewer of filth, greed, and duplicity; the Web is as tawdry as a traveling carnival's fixed game of ring toss. For all the fanfare, we're really not much different now from the way we were before the Web entered the scene. What's more, the dot-com crash at the beginning of the century proved that the early overheated claims were not just unwarranted but embarrassing.

Each statement in the above paragraph is true. But taken together and apart, they also each miss the point. They're taunts from people who think they've dodged a bullet: "Nah nah, you missed!" But they shouldn't gloat too soon. The Web will have its deepest effect as an idea. Ideas don't explode; they subvert. They take their time. And because they change the way we think, they are less visible than a newly paved national highway or the advent of wall-sized television screens. After a while, someone notices that we're not thinking about things the way our parents did.

The Web isn't entering the realm of our thoughts directly as an idea; it's getting there as a technology. Ever since Marshall McLuhan told us that the medium is the message, we're used to that: we adopt a technology and it alters the way we think just as much as an explicit philosophical credo or manifesto can. McLuhan also told us why that happens: technologies are really extensions of our own bodies. They are, in the words of Andrew Clark, a type of "external scaffolding." Change our bodies and our ideas change; that comes with being pineal creatures. The Web is doing more than extending our bodies, however. Yes, like the telephone and fax, it's extending our senses of hearing and sight. But it's also creating a new, persistent public space where our extended bodies can go. The message of the Web as a medium is this: Ultimately, matter doesn't matter. If we can be together so successfully in a world that has no atoms, no space, no uniform time, no management, and no control, then maybe we've been wrong about what matters in the real world in the first place.

Not only can we glimpse the ideas that are the message of this medium but we can find they have a certain familiarity. And because of that, although we don't know what the Web will look like as it develops, we have solid grounds for optimism. Hope is warranted. We should give in to it.

While I'm online, my real-world chair creaks and my real-world radio vibrates the real-world air. If I buy something online, my real-world bank transfers real-world money, and if

I sell child pornography online, my real-world butt is likely to sit in a real-world jail cell for real-world years. No matter what virtual personae I may create, they are all personae of the person typing the words, a person with a social security number and a single, fleshy body that is not nearly as nimble as its Web voices are. This one, single, indivisible person is having his ideas changed by the Web. And because we are the identical people offline as online, those ideas will have effects in the real world.

We're not just curious about this. We're worried and hopeful at the same time. We've seen some effects of the Web on the real world already, and they're mixed. Yes, the only independent radio station in Kosovo was able to continue transmitting by moving its signal over the Internet so it could be rebroadcast back into the country. Yes, after the World Trade Center was destroyed, the Web provided the world with a person-to-person news network that delivered good information and even some consolation. But we've also seen our economy kicked around in part because of inflated hopes for a new way of building businesses. We've seen far more efficient supply chains in business but also far more time wasted by people surfing the Web for porn while at work. It's natural, therefore, to ask the question about the Web's effect on the real world with some true urgency and perhaps bated breath.

Unfortunately, answers can't come quickly. The Web is indeed speeding up the pace by enabling ideas to be heard and discussed faster than ever before, but it takes more than a "meme" or an "idea virus" to work through the implications of a change in bedrock concepts. It can take generations to transform our understanding of ourselves and our world.

Even if these ideas moved at the speed of electrons, we would still have to wait to see how they will affect the real world, for this depends at least as much on politics as on understanding. For example, we can't know how much of the Web's attitude towards open access to creative materials will affect the real world's attitude without knowing how the courts will rule and how the generational politics will play out. Even the effect of something as simple as email is still being felt in the real world of business as some meetings are made obsolete and all others are influenced by the direct, equal-to-equal communication that email affords. Exactly how email will affect the organization of companies depends on everything from what corporate policies are set in place and how much managers sound like jerks when responding to email from their subordinates. Nevertheless, it is a certainty that our experience of the Web is affecting our real-world institutions and behaviors, for inevitably we carry off the Web the lessons we learned on it.

We're not morons about this, of course. Having learned from the Web that distance doesn't matter, we don't think we can move our furniture from Albuquerque to Azerbaijan just by clicking on a link. We have to look instead at relatively small changes that perhaps portend what's to come. The concrete effects of ideas are usually based on our concrete interactions. For example, the invention of money affected us not directly through the abstract idea that goods and services could be exchanged through an intermediary class of objects; instead, it took farmers who were experiencing a new type of social inter-course, selling eggs to someone who would resell them to someone else. So, if we want to see the influence of the ideas changed by the Web, we should look at changes in behavior.

For example, the kids who are posting reviews at Amazon aren't thinking about their relationship to the world. But they are implicitly seeing the world as a collection of people grouped by what they like to read. This is the opposite of thinking about the world as land masses that group people through the tyranny of distance. Does this mean that there will be no more wars? Of course not. But it would be just as foolish to think that our children's view of the world as one big book club won't affect how they engage with the world when their time comes.

The Web teaches us that massive projects can succeed without centralized management and control. Does this mean that the next time a city wants to build a Hoover-style dam, it will just open up some acreage and hope the citizenry will show up with cement mixers and waders? No, but when it comes to large systems that are intended to be creative—say, a knowledge management system for a large organization—our experience of the Web will encourage us to cut the reins and to value the voices around us.

The Web teaches us that we can be part of the largest public ever assembled and still maintain our individual faces. But this requires living more of our life in public. On the Web, the notion of a diary has been turned inside out: weblogs are public diaries. It is likely that the neat line we draw between our public and private selves in the real world will continue to erode, grain by grain. For example, business cards sometimes contain a link to a home page that is usually more personal than a business card. In small ways like this, the Web's notion of public and private is changing the line between our public and private lives.

The Web's linked architecture is getting us used to the idea that we should be able to find more information about everything and anything. We expect the web of links to be inexhaustible. We already see in the real world more layers of information in everything from "pop-up" music videos and DVDs having commentary tracks to the new, busy look of newspapers as they cram pages with small boxes of loosely joined information.

The Web has taught us that, to find appreciative readers, an author doesn't have to be one of the handful of writers who can fit through the eye of a publishing house. Someone wants to hear what we have to say and likes the way we say it. This will make the gap between our ownmost voice and the tinny sounds we hear coming out of our mouths at work even less supportable. The sound of the human voice is returning to work. It has always sounded in the halls, but now it will also be heard in the marketing materials that used to reek of a perfect propriety. And, after an email exchange with a really cool person at the company who has the enthusiasm of a user about the company's products, we will have no patience for the bottom-line monotone of the corporate suit, whether the naked person inside is a salesperson or a CEO.

These changes, and many others like them, will occur not for abstract reasons having to do with the dialectical development of history; rather, when you get off the trampoline, the ground doesn't feel bouncy enough. The Web is a powerful experience for many of us because it gives us a place free of what has been holding back our better selves. Much, but not all, of that experience can be transferred to the real world. A combination of habit, custom, economics, politics, and law will determine exactly how much and in what form the real world will change. We can't know whether voting online will be approved by our government and we can only guess at the effect that may have in skewing our elections this way or that. We can't know when electronic books will become affordable and truly usable, so we can't know if e-books will turn reading into a social act. We can't know if cheap batteries will be invented that will bring continuous wireless Web access to just about everyone on the globe. We're an imponderable species with an appetite for surprising ourselves.

Nevertheless, the changes we can see generally feel like a return to our best nature. This is because they are part of the overall movement of the Web, a path of return to a home that has been altered by the journey. Paradoxical? No more so than falling in love and becoming more of the person you were waiting to be.

————

Hollywood types like to talk about the "arc" of a character, by which they mean what happens to a character and the way the character develops. There's been a characteristic arc to the ideas we've been discussing throughout this book. For example, we saw that we think about space one way but experience it another: Our concept of space as an empty container divided into an abstract and uniform grid is useful for coordinating and manipulating the things of our world, but it is at odds with our everyday experience of space as a set of *places* that have meaning, character, and emotional qualities. The Web, we argued, is composed of a set of places onto which an abstract grid doesn't fit; it is thus much more like our experience of space than like our thoughts about space.

Similarly, our abstract ideas about time, matter, individuality, sociality, knowledge, and more, are out of sync with our lived experience. The Web is different enough from the real world that the mistakes we've made about the real world don't distract us there. Thus, our experience of the Web is closer to the truth of our lived experience than are our ideas about our lived experience.

We saw this in topic after topic: because there's no abstract space on the Web, we can't misconstrue the Web's spatiality the same way we've misconstrued real-world space. Web time explicitly threads our discontinuous involvement with it, so we can't misconstrue Web time as consisting of a continuous string of particularized moments. Web knowledge comes in the form of people speaking in their own voices, so we're not as tempted to seek voiceless, passionless authorities. The Web, overall, shows us more purely the truths of our human experience, truths that have been obscured by our thinking about human experience. That's why the Web—which is just a network of computers, not the fountain of youth or a cure for cancer—has excited our culture beyond any reasonable expectation: it helps to heal our alienation from our own experience. We could even formulate it as an overly tidy "law": A culture's excitement about the Web is directly proportional to that culture's alienation from its everyday experience.

That's why the Web, for all its technological newness and oddness, feels so familiar to us. And that's why it feels like a *return* even though it is the newest of the new. The Web is a return to the values that have been with us from the beginning. It is even a return to our basic self-understanding—a return from the distraction of modernism and the antihuman untruths embodied in the default philosophy we all carry with us like a hundred-pound backpack. When you set it down, you feel like you can fly.

———————

That backpack contains ideas that seem so true yet are utterly nondescriptive not only of our daily lives but of what matters to us:

In the backpack is *individualism,* the idea that we are first and foremost isolated human beings. Groups are secondary to individuals, our default philosophy says, because groups can't exist without individuals but individuals can exist without groups. But with this individualism comes a lonely selfishness that does a true disservice to the concern for others that guides our every waking moment. The Web, on the other hand, exists only because its 300 million denizens are reaching out to others. The Web is possible only as a group activity.

In the backpack is *realism* (or what some would call "materialism"), the idea that the real world is fully independent of our awareness of it. That's undeniably true: we live in a world not of our own making. But our default realism goes further than this and gives things independent of us extraordinary and unwarranted clout in all human activities: Facts trump desires, and feelings are for sissies. The Web, on the other hand, is thoroughly a creation of subjective human beings and is built not of atoms or matter or facts but of human interests.

In the backpack is *relativism,* the idea that all concepts and values depend on accidents of history and culture. This is true, but we've taken it to mean that concepts and values have no "real" value because "real" means "independent of humans": We've set the hurdle impossibly high. Therefore, with relativism comes alienation from one's own values. But the Web is a revel of values and viewpoints. The differences that supposedly disprove the worth of all values turn out on the Web to be a source of joy.

When you have finished unpacking the backpack, you may notice a lingering whiff of *solipsism,* the idea that all we can really know is what's inside our own heads. This is also true . . . if you define "know" as "to know with a psychotic degree of certainty." With solipsism comes alienation from all that we know and love outside ourselves. The Web, on the other hand, is a multibillion-point reflection on the world, on its inhabitants, and on their own reflections about the world. It is a fractal image of the world outside our own minds. To a solipsist, the Web is the most irrelevant contraption ever invented.

There's an arc to what's been placed in our backpack. The beliefs are true as far as they go. But they carry value judgments that fly in the face of who we are and who we are happiest being. Yes, we're individuals, but we're at our best when we acknowledge our deep attachment to the others of our world. Yes, the world is independent of us, but we're at our best when we work the stuff of the world to enrich our common potential. Yes, our values and concepts are relative to our culture and language, but we're at our best when we build on that collective work, not when we vainly try to flee from it like a child attempting to jump over his own shadow. These beliefs put together and shorn of their negative valuations say something quite commonsensical and quite true: We are creatures in a shared world not of our making, and we're in it not simply as bodies but as people who care about ourselves and others; we understand our world based on the hard work and poetry of those who went before us.

———————

Being a creature who cares about others is a precondition for being moral. This is reflected on the Web, although in an odd way, for if you had to guess based solely on random browsing, you'd probably conclude that the Web's politics tends towards the hysterically conservative and its moral values tend towards the pornographic. But there is no single "Web morality." Although the geek ethos gave the Internet a certain set of starting values—it favored openness of information and self-reliance, for example, without which the Web could not have been built—the moral sway of the geeks waned precisely when having an email address that ended in "aol.com" lost its stigma. You will find politics and morality of every sort on the Web, a fact that's more important than the particular moral values of the Net's founders way back when. But beneath this Babel of values we can hear something that should give us heart: the Web's architecture itself is fundamentally moral.

At first glance, this claim is hardly credible. If anything, the Web has unleashed a torrent of scams and filth that our species will not be putting on its résumé. And on the Web moral questions seem to come unglued, resulting in endlessly roiling controversies. But this ungluing is instructive. Let's look at two examples.

In May 1999, ThirdVoice, a Singapore-based software company, announced a new product. In typical Web fashion, the product was free. And controversial. ThirdVoice (the name of the software product as well as the company) attached itself invisibly to your browser. The only sign of its presence was an extra button on your browser and some extra menu entries . . . until you went to a Web site and discovered "sticky notes" on it that you'd never seen before. Only users of ThirdVoice could create the sticky notes, and only users of ThirdVoice could see them.

If it were simply a matter of ThirdVoice users being able to deface other people's sites, the condemnation would have been unambiguous. But it was much more complex than that because the sticky notes weren't technically attached to the pages they appeared on. When a ThirdVoice user created a sticky note, it was stored on a server that ThirdVoice owned. If you had attached their software to your browser, every time you went to a site, your browser looked on the ThirdVoice server to see if anyone had left notes for that site. If so, ThirdVoice worked with the browser to make it look as if the notes were on the Web site being visited. The notes therefore didn't change a single bit of the page they seemed attached to. Yet, if you were maintaining, say, the Apple site, you might not have been thrilled with the idea that your page could look as if it were filled with notes that could have contained lies, slander, racist comments, and rabid misinformation about the Apple Macintosh. And while your site would look that way only to someone who had voluntarily downloaded the ThirdVoice software, when the product was launched it seemed to be such a good idea that some people thought it "inevitable" that ThirdVoice would become a standard part of every browser and thus everyone would see the comments left by others.

I started collecting emails and discussion group postings on the topic and found the following analogies from various people:

The notes are like yellow sticky notes (so they're ok).

The notes are like graffiti (so they're bad).

No, it's like you painting my house a new color because you don't like the old one.

No, it's like me wearing sunglasses to change the way your house looks to me.

No, it's like posting reviews on the door of a restaurant . . . except you can only see them if you wear special sunglasses . . . and they're not really on the door of the restaurant, they're actually holograms projected from a satellite into the sunglasses of passersby . . . but they're indistinguishable from real reviews . . . and maybe the human eye will evolve so that you see them whether you put on the sunglasses or not . . .

. . . and on and on and on.

The controversy was never settled, although it lost much of its urgency once it became clear that ThirdVoice wasn't going to catch on. Indeed, the company closed its doors in 2001. But the arc of the discussion is familiar; it surfaced again with Napster, where the analogies were batted back and forth like, let's say, a shuttlecock in the world's longest game of badminton: downloading music files is like taping a song off the radio, is like shoplifting CDs, is like sharing with a friend, is like setting up a free CD store next to a for-pay music store, and so forth. In fact, much of the argument against Napster was lost before it ever arose when we accepted the phrase "intellectual property," which itself draws an analogy between real estate and works of creativity.

These arguments are not the sign of sloppy thought; quite the contrary, for they show how we think about moral issues. It's even how the legal system works, at least in the case of our second example: Bidder's Edge, Inc., a site that monitored eBay and 150 other auction sites, aggregating up-to-date information from them so that a user could find every site holding an auction for a particular product at a particular time. In effect, www.BiddersEdge.com helped users cope with the popularity of eBay and other auction sites.

Predictably, lots of people liked Bidder's Edge. Also predictably, eBay did not. As the leading online auction provider, eBay saw Bidder's Edge as a threat because it would draw customers to eBay's competitors. If you were searching for, say, a Princess Diana Beanie Baby, Bidder's Edge might tell you that although there are three such auctions at eBay, there are another two at other sites where the high bid is lower and the dolls are in better condition. And so, even more predictably, eBay sued.

It was hard to know whom to root for. As consumers, we wanted Bidder's Edge to win; not only did it enable us to find the best deals but it offered a check on eBay's budding hegemony in the world of Web consumer auctions. Besides, Bidder's Edge did only what consumers were already doing by the millions every day; that is, it searched numerous auction sites to see what was available. On the other hand, every time Bidder's Edge "pinged" eBay, eBay's servers had to provide an answer, in effect supporting Bidder's Edge with information that eBay didn't want to provide. But Kimbo Mundy, the founder of Bidder's Edge, said that his site was using only a tiny portion of the excess capacity of eBay's computers. He went on to make the point that once eBay has granted public access to information, it can't then hope to control how the public uses that information.[1] eBay replied that this public information is far and away eBay's greatest asset and it has every right to control access to it.

In April 2000, this bewildering case reached U.S. District Judge Ronald M. Whyte, who threw out six of the seven complaints by eBay, including its claims that Bidder's Edge violated its copyrights and that Bidder's Edge's searches cost eBay money. He found merit, however, in eBay's claim that Bidder's Edge was trespassing on eBay. He issued a preliminary injunction against Bidder's Edge.

Now, no matter where you stand in the controversy, Judge Whyte's decision that Bidder's Edge was trespassing on eBay is at least odd. Trespassing applies when someone willfully moves his body on to someone else's land. But eBay has no land and Bidder's Edge has no body. This couldn't literally be a case of trespassing any more than it could be a case of pickpocketing. It would appear that Bidder's Edge was found guilty by metaphor.

Yet the judge's decision doesn't seem completely off the mark because there's something about trespassing that makes sense in this case. With trespassing, the same behavior by two people can be differentiated at the discretion of the landowner: You and I both set foot on Meg's land, and she can say that you have permission but I'm a trespasser. On the Web, eBay deems it legitimate for you and me to search its site for auction information, but it also seems reasonable for eBay to decide that Bidder's Edge just isn't allowed. And yet, the more we think about it, the more confused we become. Trespassing without land. A core business asset that's also public. Public information that can be controlled as if it were private. The situation is just too peculiar. (In March 2001, Bidder's Edge settled the case and closed down its Web site. Trespassing in this case carried the death penalty.)

In both the ThirdVoice and Bidder's Edge examples, we rely on our age-old way of thinking about morality: analogies. But our thinking founders in both cases because the Web is so new and unusual that the analogies are hard to draw. We end up resorting either to bizarre analogies (such as restaurant reviews on virtual doors) about which our moral sense is unclear or to clear analogies (such as trespassing) that we aren't confident really apply.

Our default philosophy isn't comfortable with this way of proceeding, although it is by far the most common way of thinking about morality, and it works in most cases. Our default philosophy thinks that morality is really about principles, not analogies. To think about morality, we're supposed to find a principle and then apply it. Morality, we've been taught, consists of a set of rules. Follow the rights ones and you're a good person. Get them wrong or don't follow them and you're a naughty, bad, wicked, or evil person.

But where do the rules come from? The study of morality has moved in basically the same way ever since Socrates: Put a set of indisputably good actions into one bag and a set of indisputably bad ones into another, and then find a moral principle that accurately sorts the actions into the right bags. Say we come up with a principle that says an action is morally good if it increases the sum total of pleasure (or decreases pain); this is called "Utilitarianism." Sounds reasonable. So we throw examples at it to test it. How about the poor, hungry child who steals a loaf of bread from a prosperous chain store? The child alleviates a lot of pain while causing very little pain to the merchant, so Utilitarianism says to go ahead and steal the bread, and that doesn't sound unreasonable. How about "pooper scooper" laws requiring dog owners to tidy up after their pets? A little effort by dog owners makes the town much more pleasant, so that makes sense, too. Or perhaps you disagree. Perhaps you factor in the pain dogs suffer when they are no longer allowed to run free. Utilitarianism still seems to work; we're just disagreeing over how to calculate the pain and pleasure in this particular case.

Ah, but suppose our town passes a law that declares Christianity the official religion and outlaws expressions of other beliefs. Yes, the one non-Christian family in town will feel considerable pain, but the rest of the town is going to love the benefits of homogeneity—no pussyfooting around religious topics in school, no arguments about decking the town hall in Christmas lights, and so on. The town's pleasure is huge. In fact, we could just deport the non-Christian family and still be ahead in the pleasure-pain ratio. And suppose it turns out that getting rid of the "sexually deviant" and the "defectives" brings net gains in pleasure. Utilitarianism would tell us that therefore those are morally good policies. But it seems clear that this type of ethnic cleansing belongs in the bag marked "Bad Things to Do," so we will reject this simple version of Utilitarianism because it counts as moral actions that we *know* are immoral.[2]

Our moral reasoning thus turns out not to work the way our default philosophy says it does. Rather than first finding the principles we should uphold, we decide which principles to accept by consulting our preexisting moral sense. If someone proposes a principle that says what's right is wrong and what's wrong is right, we'll reject the principle. Principles come late to the party. They are ways of expressing and making sense of our moral intuitions.

Note, however, that this is a dangerous idea.[3] We know all too well that cultures have "intuited" as proper practices from infanticide to slavery that we now perceive as abhorrent. We have suffered through times when it has been "self-evident" that women ought to stay in the kitchen, that animals should be tortured for sport, that entire continents are "dark" and need the white man's enlightenment. In a hundred years, our descendents may look on our behaviors with the same sense of shameful wonder as we look upon our slave-holding predecessors. "They used to *eat* animals!" they may exclaim. "They made children sit in classrooms for twelve years!" they may say. "They used internal combustion engines and air conditioners!" "They had this weird notion of 'fun'! Think of all the time they wasted!" "They actually felt worse about the starving family next door than about the starving family continents away. Can you believe Grandma and Grandpa's distanceism?!" We may be tomorrow's moral monsters. History teaches us no less.

We needn't feel completely unmoored. Morality arises only because we share a world with others about whom we care. If we shared a world with creatures about whom we cared nothing, we could do whatever we wanted without feeling any moral constraints. Want bread? Steal Tom's. Want sex? Rape Pat. But we recognize that others have interests like ours and that their interests are as important to them as ours are to us. This doesn't tell us exactly how to balance each person's interests and needs, and what principles to apply to decide the hard cases, but without this fundamental caring and recognition of others, morality wouldn't arise for us any more than it does for an infant or a goldfish.

The sharing that counts isn't the sharing of the same spherical tract of land. Geography isn't what holds us together. On the Web, there's no land beneath us, no planet spinning us, no sky beckoning to us. All that holds us together is what we're interested in, what matters to us, what we care about. The Web gives us nowhere to hide from our caring nature, no convenient mistake by which we can claim to be stuck with other people against our will. Matter drops out and we're left with ourselves and nothing else.

There's that arc again. Our default philosophy says that we are primarily individuals who happen to share a planet. But we don't live that way. Our moral nature shows otherwise. Our conversational nature shows otherwise. The Web comes along and makes clear that our default philosophy is just plain wrong. The Web helps us to embrace without embarrassment who we really are. It returns us to ourselves. It arches over the alienation we've been taught to take as a sign of tough-mindedness. The Web's movement is towards human authenticity.

"Authenticity" is one of those tough terms. It seems to mean something quite distinct and identifiable, but it also has a certain fragility, as if examining it too closely would cause it to melt under the lights. There is a seeming paradox at its heart, for it says that we can be who we are or not be who we are. The first seems redundant, the second impossible. But that's just because humans are human in a different way than rocks are rocks. Part of what we are is how we understand ourselves: We can understand ourselves in a way that is false to who we are as individuals or as people. But there's more to the story than that, for being inauthentic isn't simply being mistaken. It means living in a way that's at a distance from who we really are. It means being alienated from ourselves.

As countless poems, songs, novels, and works of philosophy have told us, we live in an age of alienation. Our default philosophy's beliefs about the nature of the real world and our relationship to that world don't adequately describe their subject. They paint a picture of us primarily as individuals, yet we are possible only when we are embedded in a community and a shared history. They paint the real as that which exists independent of us when what counts most to us is the world in its involvement with us. They paint consciousness as a type of bodiless knowing when we can think and feel only because we are our bodies. They paint time and space as measurable, abstract quantities when we experience them as our life spent in places with significance to us. But these beliefs are not merely mistakes like thinking that Jupiter has twelve small moons instead of thirteen. We view our lives through these beliefs: We think consciousness is a layer separable from our bodies, we think we project meanings onto the world, we think that realism should have moral force over all other moods. We can experience our world in a way that's false to our experience because we are

such complex creatures and have such a crazy self-aware awareness. Thus our default philosophy becomes something we live,
and we become alienated from our own nature, and we become
inauthentic.

There is in addition an alienation built into human existence.
We are creatures of passion and care born into a world not of
our making. At the heart of our default philosophy's overly
emphatic realism is a truth so deep that it's completely obvious:
The world doesn't care about us. The ocean that drowns us
doesn't care if we sink or swim, the ground that buries us can't
tell the difference between a sinner and a saint. Even the atoms
that make us up will go on their way unchastened once our bodies dissolve. If God gave us this world, the world is still the
given into which we were unwillingly born.

But the Web is ours. Like a book, we are writing it, filling its
pages with passionate views of our lives and world. Like a conversation, we are talking across and despite the distances about
what matters to us, from the amusing to the life-enhancing to
the death-defying. Like a language, the Web enables us to meet
not in distance but in meanings. Like a world, it is an abiding
place where we can accomplish together whatever it is that our
caring natures put us up to.

Unlike the real world, though, there's no nature in this new
world, nothing into which we are born except what we have
made for one another. Unlike the real world, we aren't thrown
into it but enter voluntarily, the clicking of our mice like knocks
on a door. Unlike the real world, the new world of the Web is
thoroughly and inalienably ours.

———————

Being on the Web doesn't make an individual more authentic. We know that people use the Web to fool themselves and others. Any page or chat room persona may be as dishonest as a senior manager's expense report. If the Web is bringing us closer to human authenticity, it is doing so at the level of our species, not individuals. If space aliens want to learn who we are as humans, they shouldn't read our newspapers and they certainly shouldn't watch our TV programs. They should browse the Web.

It is not a perfect reflection. For one thing, since anyone with an email program and a mailing list can spam millions of people, a Web-only view of us would overemphasize the importance of annoyance marketing. On the other hand, the prevalence of pornography probably represents our dirty, dirty selves more accurately than the transcripts of all our polite, sexless office conversations. Most of all, the Web is a more honest—because unguarded—reflection of what we are like when we seek one another out without the limitations the real world imposes on us. It's not always a pretty picture, but it's a hell of a lot more fun than posing in your prom outfit all your life.

The Web is not the messiah dressed in cables and bits. It does not signal the apocalypse. It does not even make us all millionaires. But it is also more than merely another new technology.

If it were merely a technology that patched us all together, it would be a big deal, although merely the latest in a history of technological big deals. But there is something special about it, for it not only gives everyone on the planet who has a computer (or, in the age of wirelessness, a Web-enabled cell phone) access to everyone else similarly connected, it also creates a new, persistent public world that accumulates value with every interaction. It's a world that we build simply by using it, and what is of worth stays and adds to the Web's overall worth. We've never before had a second world, much less one so widely accessible and so logarithmically valuable.

But that is merely the infrastructure, or, more exactly, the opportunity. Once we are on the Web, we find the ground has dropped out from beneath us. The normal constraints, on which we have built the common sense that guides us, fall away. And so we improvise and invent. Our most important constructions are not the pages we put up or the stories we tell or the poems we record or the videos we post. Far more important is the way we reinvent what it means to be together as human beings. We are sharing this new world not because we have to but because we want to. We are sharing this world not because we find ourselves next to someone due to the inevitable accident of proximity but because we have chosen to join with someone based on the common ground of shared passions.

In fact, it's not quite true to say that we're sharing the new world of the Web because we want to. We're sharing the new world of the Web because that's the type of creature we are. We are sympathetic, thus moral. We are caring, thus social. These facts are easy to miss in the real world where we can blame space and geography for our involvement with others. On the Web we have no one to blame but ourselves.

After hallmark.com hires a new platoon of Web designers, and after AOL/Time-Warner's shareholders discover that there is no such thing as "location location location" on the Web,

.Zannah will still be revealing what she wants to reveal in a casually ironic way. Helmig will still be offering updated handholding for people who have networking problems. The people at VolvoSpy.com will still be arguing the advantages of DTC versus STC. The Web is fundamentally theirs. That is, the Web is fundamentally ours.

That—not dot-coms, mergers, or the endless lust for dirty pictures—will draw the arc of the Web.

NOTES

PREFACE

1. The official Monty Python home page is www.pythononline.com. The Ann Elk script can be found at www.montypython.net/scripts/dinosaur.php. Surely Monty Python owns the copyright on the Ann Elk sketch.

CHAPTER ONE

1. Dave Bryan, "Parent: Teen Accused of Threatening Columbine Student Was 'Bored,'" AP, December 18, 1999; http://www.newstimes.com/archive99/dec1899/naf.htm.

2. In 1978, former San Francisco supervisor Dan White murdered Mayor George Moscone and supervisor Harvey Milk. White was found guilty of involuntary manslaughter rather than first-degree murder because the jury accepted that he was operating under "diminished capacities." According to the Urban Legends Reference Page, the Twinkie defense was never actually offered. Instead, an expert witness testified that White's abandoning of his usual health-food regime was evidence of his deep depression. The witness did not claim that eating junk food *caused* the depression. Barbara and David Mikkelson, 1999, http://www.snopes2.com/spoons/fracture/twinkie.htm.

3. Sherry Turkle has written two excellent and prescient books on the nature of the self online: *The Second Self: Computers and the Human*

Spirit (New York: Simon & Schuster, 1984) and *Life on the Screen: Identity in the Age of the Internet* (New York: Simon & Schuster, 1995).

4. Ten Thousand Villages has a Web presence too, of course, at http://www.tenthousandvillages.com/.

5. http://www.i5ive.com/article.cfm/quilts_and_quilting/37365

6. http://charlotte.med.nyu.edu/jamesdj/photos/crafts.html

7. Lawrence Biemiller, "Lonely and Unhappy in Cyberspace? A New Study Prompts On-Line Debate," Chronicle of Higher Education 45, no. 4 (1998).

8. John Schwartz, "Who Says Surfers Are Antisocial?" *New York Times*, October 26, 2000.

9. Ibid., citing Robert Kraut.

10. Maura Kelly, "Your Boss May Be Monitoring Your Email," *Salon* (December 8, 1999), http://www.salon.com/tech/feature/1999/12/08/email_monitoring/index.html.

11. Thomas York, "Invasion of Privacy? E-Mail Monitoring Is on the Rise," *InformationWeek* (February 21, 2000).

12. Fred Kaplan, "Words That Haunt: Student's Dark Humor Brings a Hospitalization Order," *Boston Globe,* May 2, 2000.

13. Sally Jacobs, "After Political Storm, N.H. Ponders," *Boston Globe,* January 12, 2001.

14. http://www.stormwerks.com/linked/

15. http://www.stormwerks.com/found2/

16. The distance from Boston to Akron is 640 miles. Hamlet can be done in 625 miles.

17. William Joe Simonds, "The Boulder Canyon Project: Hoover Dam," http://www.usbr.gov/history/hoover.htm.

CHAPTER TWO

1. Cheswick's home page is http://www.cheswick.com/ches/index.html. The McCollough Effect can be found at http://www.cheswick.com/ches/me/index.html.

2. Typing in "cheswick" now takes you to the Cheswick family's home page; there you'll find a link to Bill's page.

3. In the fall of 2000, Ches's group was spun out into the Lumeta Corporation, which commercializes these maps and other Internet analysis services. Ches is chief scientist (http://www.lumeta.com/). This infor-

mation about Cheswick's map first appeared in a short article I wrote for *Wired* in 1998. It can be found online at http://www.wired.com/wired/archive/6.12/scenic.html.

4. After I wrote this chapter, but before Tim Bray read it, he invited me to become a member of the board of directors of the company he founded to commercialize this mapping technology. I accepted the invitation.

5. For an academic view of this, see my article, "Three Types of *Vorhandenheit*," *Research in Phenomenology* 10 (1980).

6. In his excellent book, *Scrolling Forward* (Arcade Publishing, 2001), David Levy takes issue with this point as expressed in a small article I wrote for *Wired* (August 1996): 112. He says that documents are "things that speak" for us, an eloquent expression that has much merit. But that is itself a highly elastic definition that doesn't help us sort through borderline examples.

7. Michael Heim is the author of *Electric Language: A Philosophical Study of Word Processing* (New Haven: Yale University Press, 1987); *The Metaphysics of Virtual Reality* (New York: Oxford University Press, 1994); and *Virtual Realism* (New York: Oxford University Press, 1997).

8. http://cyberforum.artcenter.edu/html/summer2000/log-S5.html

9. Gaston Bachelard, *The Poetics of Space,* trans. Maria Jolas (Boston: Beacon Press, 1994).

CHAPTER THREE

1. Actually, Heraclitus said, "You cannot step twice into the same rivers; for fresh waters are ever flowing in upon you" (trans. John Burnet, 1892). Available online at http://plato.evansville.edu/public/burnet/ch3a.htm. And, just as Humphrey Bogart never actually said, "Play it again, Sam" in *Casablanca,* the phrase "Everything flows" *(panta rei)* doesn't show up in any of the extant fragments from Heraclitus. Plato, however, says that that's what Heraclitus believed, and Aristotle backs him up. Good enough for me.

CHAPTER FOUR

1. "Among the 260 e-commerce Web sites tracked by Harris Interactive, Hallmark ranks as the 38th most popular site. That's far behind Bluemountain.com, which is ranked fourth." Jennifer Mann, "Hallmark Is Slowly Making Progress with E-Commerce," *Kansas City Star,* June 12,

2000, http://www.kcstar.com/item/pages/tech.pat,business/37748803.
612,.htm.

2. A sad coda: Blue Mountain sold itself to Excite in the fall of 1999 for
    $780,000,000 and has since lost much of its character. For the
    announcement of the sale, visit http://corp.excite.com/news/pr_991025
    _01.html.

3. http://pressroom.hallmark.com/hmk_fact_sheet.html

4. http://www.kkk.org, March 2001

5. Elisabeth Kübler-Ross's book *On Death and Dying* (New York: Scribner,
    1969) was a cultural phenomenon that greatly lowered the barriers
    against talking about dying. She is perhaps most vividly known for her
    identification of the five steps of grieving.

6. Reported by Marina Streznewski in an email to the author, January 2001.
    She heard Tufte say this in a presentation. (Edward Tufte is the author of
    the classic book *The Visual Display of Quantitative Information,* 2d ed.
    [Cheshire, Conn.: Graphics Press, 2001]).

7. Robert Venturi, *Complexity and Contradiction in Architecture,* illustrated
    by Vincent Scully, Jr. (New York: Museum of Modern Art, 1966); Robert
    Venturi, Denise Scott Brown, and Steven Izenour, *Learning from Las
    Vegas* (Cambridge: MIT Press, 1972).

8. http://www.smokinggun.com

9. http://www.zeldman.com/ad.html

10. http://members.nbci.com/_XOOM/primall/mahir/index.html

11. It turns out that the site was in fact the "mirror" of a page that Mahir had
    put up the previous year. Someone discovered it and liked it enough to
    make a copy on a different site. The copy wasn't identical, however; the
    perpetrator spiced it up by adding comments such as "I like sex" and
    inserting "nice nude girls" into the list of things Mahir likes to photo-
    graph.

12. http://www.ikissyou.org/

13. http://www.nytimes.com/yr/mo/day/news/financial/ford-suv.html

14. http://www-forums.shell.com/forums/main.cfm? ForumNumber=7&
    CFApp=2&siteid=1160&entry=1

15. Posted February 7, 2001.

16. Telephone conversation with the author, May 8, 2001.

17. Posted February 16, 2001.

18. Posted February 26, 2001.

19. *Letitia Baldridge's New Complete Guide to Executive Manners* (New
    York: Rawson Associates, 1993), 114–115.

20. Ibid., 128.

21. Jupiter Media Metrix study, reported in *InformationWeek* (March 22, 2001).

CHAPTER FIVE

1. Jerry Michalski in his closing keynote at the Connections conference in 1998, as reported in an article by Deborah Carter, "Weaving a New Societal Fabric," http://www.digitaledge.org/connections98/michalski. html. This phrase, or one like it, will very likely figure in Michalski's new book from the Harvard Business School Press, due in the spring of 2002, provisionally titled *The Big Flip: Reversing 50 years of Consumerism.*

2. http://weblog.mercurycenter.com/ejournal/

3. http://www.lockergnome.com

4. David Reed and David Weinberger, "Reed's Law: An Interview," *Journal of the Hyperlinked Organization* (January 19, 2001), http://www.hyper-org.com/backissues/joho-jan19–01.html#reed.

5. Metcalfe's Law says that the value of the network is N * (N – 1), where N is the number of connections, since you can't call yourself without getting a busy signal. And David Reed responded to a draft of this manuscript with the following email:

> A numerical quibble—since you take pains to be precise about the number of pairwise connections in a set of 15, giving the correct answer, 210, which is n(n–1) or n^2-n, you should probably be precise about the number of non-trivial groups in a set of 15. Since the 2^n formula includes the following trivial subsets in its count, you might want to give the answer 32,752.
>
> - the "empty set," which is the group with no members at all, and
>
> - the 15 "singleton sets," which are the groups containing one member.
>
> In general, the precise formula for non-trivial subsets is 2^n – n – 1, but that grows just as fast as 2^n.
>
> Some pain-in-the-ass literalist reader or editor will claim you got the math wrong and miss the real point.

6. http://www.amazon.com/exec/obidos/tg/cm/member-reviews/-/A2VCGJLKGK2WJJ/102–3618926–6815342?desc=full

7. After I wrote this, AskJeeves switched to a different provider. Ah, the Web.

8. Conversation with the author. See "When Q&A Goes Global," *Journal of the Hyperlinked Organization* (October 20, 2000), http://www.hyper-org.com/backissues/joho-oct20–00.html.
9. http://www.shunn.net/okay/
10. http://safe.millennium.berkeley.edu/

CHAPTER SIX

1. http://dannyreviews.com/h/Inventing_Middle_Ages.html
2. http://dannyreviews.com/h/An_Introduction_to_Modern_Political_Theory.html
3. http://dannyreviews.com/IFAQ.html
4. http://www.nybooks.com/nyrev/about.html; circulation of the *New York Review of Books* includes only paid subscribers. Further, because the *New York Review* comes out many times a year, an accurate comparison would multiply the circulation by the number of issues. The relevant point of comparison is probably how many people read a particular review in the *New York Review* and on Danny's page. Danny reviews about fifty books a year. Since he has 1,350,000 page impressions per year, each review is read by 27,000 people on average. If we had some way of gauging how many reviews readers of the *New York Review* actually read in each issue, we could make the comparison. In any case, Danny's readership is less than the *New York Review*'s but is still substantial.
5. http://dannyreviews.com/IFAQ.html
6. http://danny.oz.au/danny/index.html
7. http://codeguru.earthweb.com/cgi-bin/bbs/wt/showprofile.pl? User =Iouri
8. http://www.nbcc.org.au/
9. http://www.nbcc.org.au/pages/nbabout.htm
10. http://www.nbcc.org.au/pages/support/wwwboard.htm
11. Herbert A. Simon and Associates, "Decision Making and Problem Solving," in *Research Briefings 1986: Report of the Research Briefing Panel on Decision Making and Problem Solving,* © 1986 by the National Academy of Sciences (Washington, D.C.: National Academy Press, 1986). Reprinted at http://www.dieoff.org/page163.htm.
12. http://www.dmreview.com/editorial/dmreview/print_action.cfm?EdID=2417
13. http://www.gri.org/pub/oldcontent/tech/e+p/gastips/new/gtipsf95new_1.html
14. http://www.autonomy.com/autonomy/dynamic/autopage520.shtml

15. http://www.bently.com/articles/997mcm.asp
16. A version of these comments was published in the *Harvard Business Review* (September 2001) under the title "Garbage In, Great Stuff Out," 30–32.
17. James Watson, *The Double Helix: A Personal Account of the Discovery of the Structure of DNA* (New York: New American Library, reissued 1991).
18. Thomas Kuhn, *The Structure of Scientific Revolutions,* 3d ed. (Chicago: University of Chicago Press, 1996).
19. Raymond Kurzweil, *The Age of Spiritual Machines* (New York: Penguin Books, 1999).
20. Ibid., 105.
21. Ibid., 127–129. All emphasis is Kurzweil's.
22. Douglas Hofstadter, *Gödel, Escher, Bach: An Eternal Golden Braid* (New York: Basic Books, 1979).
23. Douglas Hofstadter, "A Conversation with Einstein's Brain," in *The Mind's I,* ed. Douglas Hofstadter and Daniel Dennett (New York: Basic Books, 1981), 353–373.
24. Perhaps because "A Conversation with Einstein's Brain" is written in the form of a dialogue, it's hard to pin down Hofstadter's precise point of view on the thought experiment he proposes. The conclusion Achilles and the Tortoise explicitly agree on is that they will not shun the term *I* but "won't imbue it with such 'soulful' meanings as" they have "heretofore tended to do" (456). They get to this point by imagining that many copies of a book of Achilles's brain are printed, each claiming to be Achilles. Achilles says "The mere fact that it utters such things doesn't mean that it has 'real feelings', and perhaps even more to the point, the mere fact that I, Achilles, utter such things, doesn't really mean I am feeling anything" (456–457). That Achilles claims at the end of the thought experiment that he may not have feelings, should, in my view, be taken as evidence that the interpretation of the experiment has gone awry.
25. John R. Searle, "Minds, Brains and Programs," in *The Behavioral and Brain Science,* vol. 3 (Cambridge: Cambridge University Press, 1980); reprinted in *The Mind's I,* ed. Douglas Hofstadter and Daniel Dennett (New York: Basic Books, 1981), 353–373.
26. Ibid., 356.
27. Ibid., 367.
28. Andrew Clark, *Being There: Putting Brain, Body, and World Together Again* (Cambridge: MIT Press, 1998).
29. Once again, I have to acknowledge my debt to Martin Heidegger, whose critique of traditional (and especially philosophical) knowledge informs this chapter. Oddly, one of Heidegger's two great weaknesses is that in his

major works he did not write about the body as an essential part of the human condition. (The other weakness is that he was a Nazi.)

CHAPTER SEVEN

1. *inFORM: The Vax and Alpha Migration Magazine,* no. 11 (May/June 1996), http://www5.compaq.com/inform/issues/issue11/issue–11.html.
2. Colonel Mark B. Roddy, "Data Warehousing: A New Tool for Maintainers," http://www3.ncr.com/govmrkts/whitepaper/moadwfnl. htm.
3. http://www.cisco.com/warp/public/749/ar2000/low/financials/ notes_consolidated_statements.html
4. http://www.howstuffworks.com/router6.htm
5. For more information see G. J. C. Lokhorst and Timo T. Kaitaro, "The Originality of Descartes's Theory about the Pineal Gland," *Journal for the History of the Neurosciences* 10, no. 1 (2001), http://www.eur.nl/fw/staff/lokhorst/pineal.html.
6. Nicholas Negroponte, *Being Digital* (New York: Vintage Books, 1995), 14.
7. Ibid., 11–12.
8. Optical fiber works differently. In that case, timing pulses are sent at frequent enough intervals to prevent the bits from getting out of synch enough to cause "drifting." Thanks to Mike O'Dell, former senior vice president and Chief Scientist at UUNet, for carefully explaining many of these issues to me. All errors are due to the thickness of my skull.
9. There are actually different protocols. The HCDL protocol looks for 0111110; others work differently.
10. All examples from *WordWays* 34, no. 1 (February 2001). A. Ross Eckler, editor and publisher, Spring Valley Road, Morristown, NJ 07960.
11. Information science, created in the late 1940s by Claude Shannon and Warren Weaver to explore how a particular pattern of bits can be replicated at a destination most efficiently, will tell you that bits can be understood apart from what they stand for. Instead, all we need to know is how many possible configurations of bits there are. This is why information science is irrelevant to understanding what most of us mean by "information."
12. Obviously, some information on many pages is automatically generated by machines; for example, the flight schedules at a travel site are not generated by hand. Nevertheless, these machine-generated contents are generally embedded in pages that have been written by humans for humans.
13. http://www.asiaonline.net.hk/~tfwong/winona/

14. Stephen Jay Gould, *The Mismeasure of Man,* rev. ed. (New York: W. W. Norton, 1996).

CHAPTER EIGHT

1. In a conversation with the author, May 2000.
2. To meet these types of objections, Utilitarianism has been amended and patched over the years so that it's much more sophisticated than I'm making it out to be. But I'm only using it as an example of moral reasoning.
3. It is also an oversimplified idea. In fact, we don't merely close our eyes and intuit a judgment. We sometimes engage in a spirited conversation that may change our intuitions because of what we have been brought to think or feel. Further, there are tremendous difficulties with proposing intuitions as a basis for morality, especially if you are aiming at moral certitude as philosophers generally have. Even if you are aiming lower, as Robert Nozick says in *Invariances: The Structure of the Objective World* (Cambridge: Belknap Press of Harvard University Press, 2001), 125, "Philosophers who give great weight to intuitions need to offer some account of why such intuitions are reliable and are to be trusted." Elsewhere, I would argue for "sympathy" as the basis of morality, that is, the ability to turn towards the world with others, letting the world matter to you as it matters to others. This type of sympathy—a type of caring—is, I believe, arguably a requirement for moral behavior. And it is connected imperfectly to our intuitions. Nevertheless, I am convinced that moral reasoning—which is not the same thing as moral philosophizing, for better or worse—proceeds from intuitions, not principles.

ACKNOWLEDGMENTS

THIS BOOK WAS ENABLED by a handful of people and made better by many others.

It was enabled by David Miller and Lisa Adams of the Garamond Agency, who encouraged me to pursue this oddball theme because it was what my writing and thinking kept coming back to. They never gave me false encouragement, especially when they patiently read drafts that meandered down dead-ends, and thus their true encouragement was ever more meaningful. They also forced me to learn ways of telling this story that I hadn't considered before.

It was enabled by Amanda Cook, my editor at Perseus Books, whose advice was crystal clear and illuminating. The entire crew at Perseus has been a delight to work with.

It was enabled by Professor Joseph Fell at Bucknell University and Professor Graeme Nicholson at the University of Toronto, although neither knows this. Professor Fell made philosophy vital. Professor Nicholson generously guided me through a graduate program many years ago, and showed me that thinking requires kindness.

This book was enabled by my family. Our two younger children, Leah and Nathan, not only put up with my absence from family functions but heard portions of the book, commented with precision, and laughed at the right places. (Our oldest daughter, Jennie, is off on her own, but her independence and passion are always an inspiration.) My wife, Ann Geller, should have been the worst possible reader of drafts, for she's a philosophy Ph.D. who loves me. Nevertheless, her comments were invaluable and I can't conceive of having written this book, or of having a life, without her.

This book was improved by dozens of people who read drafts of it online as I wrote it. Juliette Chatelain deserves mention for her own beautifully written, deep commentary. And a special acknowledgement must be made of Halley Suitt, whose persistence and consistently helpful comments were more important than she knows, as was her enthusiasm during times when I needed it most and deserved it least.

Many other people have contributed to this book. Michael O'Dell helped me understand router technology. Chris "RageBoy" Locke did what a real friend should do: tell me when I'm full of crap while simultaneously cheering me on. My in-laws, Marvin and Virginia Geller, made me feel comfortable in their summer home with our extended family even as I literally closed the door on them for hours and hours on end.

Especially because I wrote this book online with participation from a Web community, the only parts of the book that we can be certain are fully and completely mine are the mistakes, errors, omissions, and parts that are written badly.

David Weinberger
September 25, 2001
self@evident.com
http://www.smallpieces.com

INDEX

Assumptions, 5, 8, 50, 97,
151, 154, 167
Athens, 129, 140
Attention span, 69
Auctions, 4, 86, 186. *See also*
eBay
Australia, I-Source National
Breast Cancer Centre
(NBCC), 124–126
Authenticity, 89, 145,
191–193, 194
Avatars, 41, 42

Bachelard, Gaston, 47
Bankruptcies, 20
Behavioral changes, 176–177
Being Digital (Negroponte),
156
Being There (Clark), 136–137
Beliefs, 140, 141, 182, 192.
See also Certainty;
Default philosophy;
Ideas; Knowledge, as jus-
tified true belief
Bell Labs, 27–28
Ben & Jerry's, 87
Benjamin, David, 103
Berners-Lee, Tim, 29, 52, 76
Bidder's Edge, Inc., 186–188
Bits, 131, 147–148, 148–150,

156–161, 163, 204(n11)
and atoms, ix, 157
as pineal-like, 161, 164
Blooper TV shows, 87
Blue Mountain Arts, 71–72,
199(chap. 4, n1), 200(n2)
Books, 36, 193
book reviews, 113–115,
121–122, 177, 202(n4)
See also E-books
Bots, 61
Boutchkine, Iouri, 122–123,
124, 126, 140, 144
Bradner, Scott, 147–148
Brains, 133–134, 136, 152,
154. *See also* Neurons
Bray, Tim, 29–32, 41,
199(n4)
Brochures, 73, 90
Brokenness, 83, 84–85. *See
also* Internet/Web, as
broken
Browsing/surfing, 35, 48–49,
68. *See also* Links
Bug's Life, A, 87
Bulletin boards, 112–113,
116, 125–126. *See also*
Discussion boards;
Forums
Burch, Hal, 28

Domain name servers, 158
Dot-com crash, 173
Double Helix, The (Watson),
    131
Dreams, 51

eBay, 3–8, 186–188
    ratings on, 5
E-books, 19, 179
Eccentricity, 93
Eckler, A. Ross, 161
E-commerce sites, 44, 93,
    199(chap. 4, n1)
Educational system, 170
Efficiency, 80, 81, 131, 144
Ego-surfing, 68
Einstein, Albert, 51–52
Email, 8(n), 10, 62, 63, 78,
    82, 91, 126, 185
    abuse of, 12–13
    and businesses, 12–13, 176,
    178
    Email complaints, 93
    mailing lists. *See* Discussion
    lists
Embodiment, 138–139
Emmons, Will, 161
Emotional qualities, 46, 47,
    92, 167
Environmental issues, 87–88

Essences, 77
Ethernet, 105
Experts, 170
Expert systems, 127

Failure(s), 73, 75, 94. *See also*
    Brokenness
Fame, 101, 103—104
    real-world vs. Web, 105
    See also Celebrities
Fashe, Fortune Adogbeji,
    89–90
FBI, 2
Fiber optics, 204(n8)
Fiction, 145, 155, 164, 165,
    170
Firings, 12–13
Ford, William C., 87
Ford Motor, 87–88
Fortune 500, 84
Forums, 15, 66, 67, 88,
    89–90, 125. *See also*
    Discussion boards
Friends, 12, 21
    online, 11

Galileo, 167
Games, 15, 48, 87
Gibson, James, 32
Gigabytes, 149

Surfing. *See* Browsing/surfing
Sympathy, 205(n)

Technologies, 132, 174, 194
Telephones, 68, 131, 160,
    163, 194
  telephone networks, 105,
    106, 107
Television, 11, 87, 96, 97, 163
Terabytes, 148–149
Thales, 129
"Thank you" messages,
    116–117
Thinking, 137, 151, 168, 180,
    188
ThirdVoice, 183–185
Thought experiments, 33–34,
    49–50, 133–134,
    135–136, 203(n24)
Threads, 60–61, 62–63, 66,
    69, 110, 111
  hyperthreads, 67–68
3Com, 105
Ticketmaster, 53
Time, 6–7, 8, 10, 24, 25, 117,
    138, 145, 174, 179–180
  and bits, 159
  control of, 59–60
  dividing/measuring, 58,
    64–65, 68–69, 192

and groups, 109–110
lived, 65, 180
story as fundamental unit
    of, 59
Today Show, 2, 3
Trespassing, 187–188
Troubleshooting, 102
Truth, 14, 129–130
  of lived experience, 180
  as representing reality,
    154
  truths of the body, 139,
    142, 145–146
  See also Certainty;
    Knowledge
Tufte, Edward, 81
Tumas, John, "Jay," 148, 149
Turkle, Sherry, 197(n3)
Twinkie defense, 2, 197(n2)

Unix directories, 16
Utilitarianism, 189, 204(n2)
UUnet, 18

Values, 155, 167, 180,
    181–182, 195
Vandalism, 39
Venturi, Robert, 82
Violence, 14, 15
VisiCalc spreadsheets, 106